SUGARPASTE
CHRISTMAS
CAKES

ANNE SMITH

MEREHURST

LONDON

I would like to thank my long-suffering husband Clive for
his continuing support. My two children Helen and David
for their love and understanding and all my family, friends
and colleagues whose interest and encouragement has been
so appreciated during the writing of this book.

All cakes have been decorated using Regalice Sugarpaste from
J. F. Renshaw Limited, Mitcham, Surrey and red colours have
been achieved using Renshaw's red compound paste.

Important
Cocktail sticks and wired flowers must only be used for
display purposes in sugarcraft. Great care should be taken
to ensure there is no possibility of any particles being eaten
accidentally. Wired flowers must always be placed in a
separate small cushion of sugarpaste or a special plastic
holder; the ends should never be inserted into the cake.

Published 1989 by Merehurst Limited
Ferry House
51-57 Lacy Road
Putney
London SW15 1PR

Reprinted 1990, 1991

© Copyright 1989 Merehurst Limited

ISBN 1 85391 053 8 (Cased)
ISBN 1 85391 194 1 (Paperback)

A catalogue record for this book is available
from the British Library

Edited by: Deborah Gray
Designed by: Clive Dorman
Cover Design by: Peter Bridgewater
Photography by: Graham Tann, assisted by Lucy Baker
Typesetting by: Vision Typesetting, Manchester
Colour separation by: J. Film, Bangkok
Printed in West Germany by Mohndruck Graphische
Betriebe GmbH

CONTENTS

INTRODUCTION

FOREWORD

It has been a delight to work on such a lovely book, and I am sure that you will be enthralled by the wealth of ideas contained in these pages. Anne Smith's artistic training shows on every page. Anne lectures in Art and Design at Bath College of Higher Education having formerly been Heaad of Arts and Crafts at a comprehensive school. She has now also turned her fertile imagination towards sugarcraft where her work has won her well-deserved acclaim. You will see examples of her fine art and painting, sculpture, design and pottery skills in cakes in this book, all skilfully employed and beautifully executed in the medium of sugarpaste.

Having said all that, this is a book for everyone to enjoy, whether you aspire to such artistic merit or whether you simply want to have a go at making an unusual Christmas cake this year. There are ideas for the novice and for those experienced in sugarcraft. There are some great ideas for those people whose Christmas revolves around the children, and many for the more mature who wish to make an elegant cake. I am quite certain that your problem on opening this book will be which cake to make for Christmas, but never mind, there's always next year.

Happy Christmas

DEBORAH GRAY
Editor

It is with pleasure that I write the foreword for the book Sugarpaste Christmas Cakes as it is indeed a delight to have yet another imaginative addition finding its way onto our bookshelves.

Anne Smith who has many years experience in cake decorating has produced a book which will provoke a lively interest and allow the imagination to soar to new heights. Anne not only has a natural ability to ice and decorate cakes, she is also a sculptor, potter and needlewoman. It is clear that these skills are adapted and in turn create fine work of great detail.

Sugarpaste is becoming increasingly popular amongst cake decorators. A good finish can be achieved without too much difficulty. However, a really smooth glossy finish with evenly rounded edges requires practice and experience. Through using this medium there is a tremendous element of fun as sugarpaste lends itself to so many uses and techniques, many of which are shown here in these various novelty cakes.

So whether it is a cake for a seasonal display or for a special event, welcome to creative fun and happy celebrations.

CARMEL A KEENS

Chief Home Economist
Tate & Lyle Sugars

SUGARPASTE RECIPES

SUGARPASTE

This is used for general purpose decoration.

15g (½oz/5 tsp) gelatine
50ml (2fl oz/¼ cup) cold water
120ml (4fl oz/⅓ cup) liquid glucose
25g (¾oz/5 tsp) glycerine
900g (2lb/6 cups) icing (confectioner's) sugar

Soak the gelatine in the cold water and place over hot water until dissolved and clear. Do not allow the gelatine to boil. Add the glycerine and glucose to the gelatine and stir until melted. Add the mixture to the sieved sugar. Knead to a soft consistency.

MODELLING PASTE

This paste is malleable and easily stretched which makes it ideal for bas relief work.

250g (9oz/2¼ cups) icing (confectioner's) sugar
15ml (1 tbsp) gum tragacanth
5ml (1 tsp) liquid glucose
30ml (6 tsp) cold water
approx. 275g (10oz) sugarpaste

Sieve the sugar with the gum tragacanth. Add the liquid glucose and cold water to the sugar and mix well. Knead to form a soft dough, then combine with an equal weight of sugarpaste. Leave for 24 hours before using. If the paste is too dry knead in a little white fat (shortening) or egg white as needed. If the paste is sticky, add a little cornflour (cornstarch).

RECIPE FOR FLOWER PASTE

There are many variations on the following recipe but this is a reliable one to start with.

400g (14oz/3½ cups) icing (confectioner's) sugar
50g (2oz/¼ cup) cornflour (cornstarch)
15ml (3 tsps) gum tragacanth
10ml (2 tsps) powdered gelatine
25ml (5 tsps) cold water
15ml (3 tsps) white fat (shortening)
10ml (2 tsps) liquid glucose
white of 1 egg, string removed

Sift together the sugar and cornflour (cornstarch) in the bowl of a heavy duty mixer. Sprinkle over the gum tragacanth. Place the mixer over a large pan of boiling water. Cover the top with a dry cloth and then with a plate. Put the cold water in a small glass bowl and sprinkle over the gelatine. Leave to sponge.

Half fill a small saucepan with water and heat to just below boiling point. Place the bowl of sponged gelatine, the container of liquid glucose and the beater from the mixer in the water. Heat gently until the gelatine is clear. Remove the bowl of gelatine from the pan and stir in the liquid glucose and the white fat (shortening). Continue to stir until the fat is melted.

When the icing (confectioner's) sugar feels warm, take the bowl off the pan of boiling water, dry the bottom and place in the mixer. Remove the beater from the other pan, dry and assemble the mixer. Add the gelatine solution and the egg white to the sugar, cover the bowl with a cloth and turn the mixer to the slowest speed. Mix until all the ingredients are combined and the paste is a dull, beige colour.

Turn the mixer to maximum and beat until the paste becomes white and stringy, about 5–10 minutes. Remove the paste from the bowl and place in a clear plastic bag. Place the bag in an airtight container and refrigerate for at least 24 hours before using.

To use the paste, cut off a small piece at a time and work the paste with your fingers until it has an elastic consistency. If the paste is dry, add more egg white or white fat (shortening); if the paste is too sticky, add a little more cornflour (cornstarch).

GELATINE PASTE

500g (1lb 2oz/4½ cups) icing (confectioner's) sugar
60ml (2fl oz/4 tbsps) cold water
5ml (1 tsp) white fat (shortening)
5ml (1 tsp) liquid glucose
15ml (3 tsp) gelatine

Soak the gelatine in the cold water and place over a pan of hot water until dissolved and clear. Do not allow the gelatine to boil.

Add the fat and glucose to the gelatine and stir until melted. Add this mixture to the sieved sugar and knead together to form a firm paste. Add a little more water if the paste is too stiff. To help the keeping quality of the paste, pat the surface all over with a little water then place in a plastic bag. Store in a cool place; it is not necessary to refrigerate this paste. Leave for 24 hours before using.

QUICK FLOWER PASTE

This paste is easier to make but the flowers will not be as strong or delicate as with regular flower paste.

225g (8oz) commercial sugarpaste
5ml (1 tsp) gum tragacanth
white fat (shortening)

Knead the sugarpaste and gum tragacanth together then add a knob of the fat to achieve an elastic consistency. Store and use as for gelatine paste.

PREPARING THE CAKE

Carefully remove the greaseproof (waxed paper) taking care not to damage the corners of the cake. Turn the cake upside-down so that the bottom of the cake provides a flat top surface. Stick the cake to the board with a little marzipan softened with warm apricot jam (jelly). If the edges of the cake do not sit level on the cake board, make a sausage of marzipan and push into the gaps with a palette knife. Fill any visible holes and repair any damaged corners with marzipan. Smooth over with a palette knife until all the damaged areas are level.

Gently heat some apricot jam (jelly), sieve and brush over the surface of the cake to ensure that the marzipan will adhere to the surface.

APPLYING THE MARZIPAN

Knead the marzipan on a clean, dry work surface until pliable using a circular motion. The edge of the paste is brought into the middle, forming pleats, while the lower surface remains quite smooth. When rolling the marzipan out, this smooth side should be uppermost.

Roll out on a surface evenly dusted with icing (confectioner's sugar). Never use flour or cornflour (cornstarch) as these can cause fermentation to occur.

When rolling out, keep the marzipan moving so that it does not stick to the work surface. Do not turn the marzipan over as for pastry, but keep this smooth surface uppermost until the desired shape and size has been achieved. Roll out the marzipan to the same shape as the cake, this makes it easier to handle when placing on the cake and avoids wastage. The use of marzipan spacers at this stage ensures that the overall thickness of the marzipan is consistent. Measure the cake with a piece of string, take it up on one side, across the top and down the other side. The marzipan should be rolled out just a little larger than this measurement.

To apply, lift up the left side of the marzipan and lay it over your right arm. Lift up your arm and drape the marzipan against the side of the cake; the right side of the marzipan should still be on the board.

Drape over the top of the cake, transfer the marzipan to the left hand and support it while you remove any air bubbles by brushing your right hand across the top of the cake.

Skirt out the corners and, using the flat of your hand, smooth the marzipan to the sides of the cake using an upward movement. If a downward movement is used, it drags the marzipan and weakens the paste causing cracks to appear on the top edges and corners. Use smoothers to eliminate any finger marks and bumps. Smooth the corners and upper edges using the warmth of your hand. Place the flat edge of a cranked palette knife against the cake at the base and cut away the excess marzipan.

APPLYING THE SUGARPASTE

The cake does not need to be covered with marzipan first. If anyone objects to the taste of marzipan, then the cake may be covered with two layers of sugarpaste instead. The first layer is usually thinner and for the best results should be allowed to skin and harden before applying the second layer. Both layers are applied in the same way.

Knead the sugarpaste as for marzipan and add any colour at this stage, see below for details.

Roll out the sugarpaste on a light dusting of icing (confectioner's sugar). Avoid using too much sugar as this will dry the paste and make it crack. Use spacers to keep the thickness of the paste uniform. Measure the cake as for marzipan and roll out the sugarpaste a little larger than the measurement.

Before applying the paste, sterilize the surface of the cake by moistening all over with a clear spirit such as gin, vodka or kirsch. Using the palm of the hand or a brush, make sure the entire surface is moist. If there are any dry areas the paste will not stick to the marzipan and could cause air bubbles.

Lift and drape the paste over the cake using the same technique as for marzipan. Skirt out the corners and smooth out any creases using an upward movement. Use smoothers to rub over the top and sides of the cake and to round the corners.

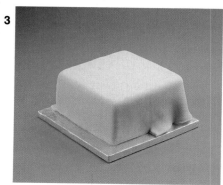

If any air bubbles have been trapped under the paste, insert a clean needle into the bubble at an angle. Smooth over with your hand to expel the air and rub with a smoother. If the pin hole is still visible, this can be easily hidden with a small dot of royal icing of the same colour piped into the hole and then wiped away to leave a smooth finish.

Use a cranked palette knife to trim away the excess paste. Smooth over the cut area. Wipe away any sugar on the board and store the cake in a dry place until the sugarpaste has skinned.

COLOURING SUGARPASTE

The colouring of any paste is better done in natural light as artificial light can affect colour perception.

Add the colour a little at a time. More colour can always be added to achieve a darker shade, whereas, if the colour is too dark, then more paste has to be added to lighten the colour resulting in wastage.

To colour a large amount of paste, divide the entire amount of paste needed into manageable portions. Colour each portion separately then knead all the portions together to blend. All the paste required must be coloured in one batch as it is almost impossible to match the colour once dried.

After kneading in the colour, cut the paste in half to see if any streaks are visible. If so, re-knead and cut again until all the streaking has disappeared.

Streaks can be used, however, to create a marbled effect which can look very attractive. To achieve this, the colour is only slightly kneaded into the paste so that when it is rolled out, the surface has a definite streaky pattern.

BASIC CHRISTMAS DECORATIONS

GARRETT FRILL

Commercial sugarpaste can be used to create a frill, but the addition of 1 teaspoon of gum tragacanth to each 450g (1lb) sugarpaste will give the paste a little extra body and avoid the frill drooping on the cake. Store the sugarpaste for at least 24 hours before using if gum has been added. Special round or straight cutters with scalloped edges are used to create the frill.

Roll the paste thinly and cut out a circle with a scalloped cutter. Remove the centre piece of paste. The size of this removed circle determines the depth of the frill. Cut out a large inside circle for a narrow frill and a small inside circle for a deeper one.

Scribe a line onto the cake where the frill is to be attached. Place the frill near the edge of the board. Put a cocktail stick, flouncing tool or anger tool (the latter two create a more definite lift) halfway up the paste and, using an index finger on top of the stick, rotate gently. As the stick moves forward over the paste it will lift up away from the board producing the frill. Repeat this action along the entire scalloped edge of the paste.

Moisten the cake below the scribed line with a little water and attach the frill. Smooth over the upper edge gently with your thumb. Raise the frill with the end of a paintbrush to give extra lift where needed. When adding the second frill, butt the edges together and turn under the extreme edge of the frill so that it appears to form a natural fold.

Several methods can be used to finish off the upper edge of the frill. Crimping can disguise a poor edge and if desired, the frill must be applied when the paste on the cake is soft. On the whole however, it is easier to avoid crimping if the base paste is already firm.

A piped edge also looks attractive, try piping a snailstrail, cross-stitch or dots. Another finish which looks very delicate is the application of small lace sections. Plunger cutter flowers can also create a pleasing effect.

Petal dusting colour may be applied to the edge of the frill or each frill can be coloured, grading the colours so that the darkest colour starts at the base of the cake.

1–3 Applying the marzipan
4 Applying sugarpaste
5 Making a Garrett frill
6 Garrett frill: application

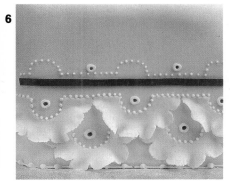

FLOWERS AND LEAVES

CHRISTMAS ROSE

Cut out a calyx using green paste. Cut five petals in white paste. Soften and thin the edges of the petals using a ball tool. Cup each petal onto foam. Lightly grease a shallow dish (or an apple tray may be used). Place the calyx into the centre of the dish. Place the petals, one at a time, onto the calyx and stick with egg white. The fifth petal should be placed overlapping the forth and tucked under the first. Pipe a small bulb of yellowish green royal icing into the centre of the flower. Insert yellow stamens around the bulb of icing, gently curving the stamen cotton with tweezers for a natural effect. When the paste is dry, lightly dust the base of the petals with green petal dust. The top edges of the rose can also be dusted a very pale pink.

VARIEGATED IVY

Ivy can be quite different in shape and colour and to achieve a realistic effect try to work from nature and not from a photograph.

One variety of ivy has a pale, golden yellow leaf with a flash of green in the centre. Another variety is completely opposite with green on the outer part of the leaf and the golden colour in the centre. There is another variety where the leaves are mostly green.

If making the variegated variety, roll out some yellow paste. Place a smaller piece of green paste onto the yellow and roll again. Place the template on top of the paste and cut the leaf out. Indent the veins using a leaf indenter. Soften and thin the edges of the leaf to give a natural shape.

Another way of achieving the variegated effect is by painting the darker tones onto the centre of the leaf with either paste or liquid food colouring. Cut out, soften edges and leave to dry as described above. When dry, using a fairly dry brush, paint in the green areas. Use a slightly paler tone of green to create a

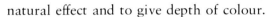

1–4 Garrett frills: seasonal applications
  5 Step-by-step holly leaves
  6 Step-by-step ivy leaves using coloured sugarpaste
  7 Step-by-step painted ivy leaves

natural effect and to give depth of colour.

For the completely green leaf, cut out, indent and soften edges then leave to dry. Mix a little green paste colour with gum arabic which will act as both a glue and a glaze. Paint the areas between the indented vein lines.

HOLLY

Cut out the leaves in a dark green paste. Soften the edges using a ball tool as for the ivy. Mark a vein line down the centre of the leaf with a veining tool. Twist and dry over a spoon handle to create natural shapes. The berries are made from small balls of red paste glazed with gum arabic, if desired.

Other leaves, berries and flowers can be made using the same principles as described above.

GUM ARABIC RECIPE

This may be used as a glaze or as a glue.

Mix the gum powder with water or rose water (rose water will give the glaze a longer shelf life). Mix three parts rose water to one part gum arabic powder.

Pour the rose water in a cup and sprinkle over the gum arabic powder. Place the cup over hot water until dissolved and clear. Strain through the toe section of a clean pair of tights (panty hose). Allow the solution to drip through.

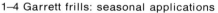

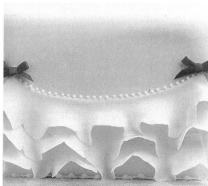

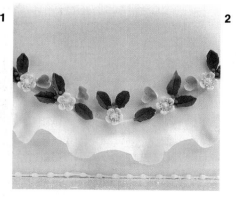

Christmas rose

Christmas rose

holly

various ivy leaves

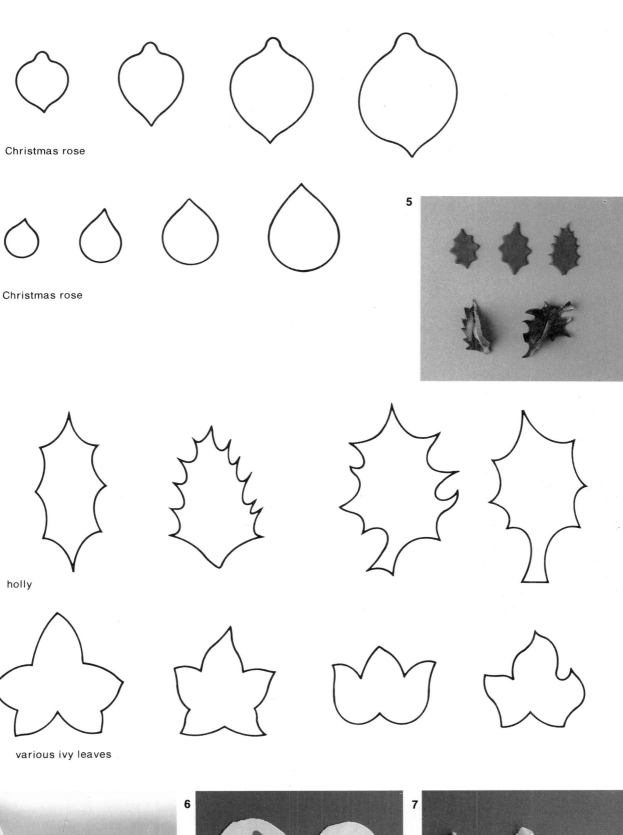

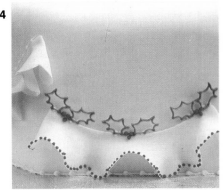

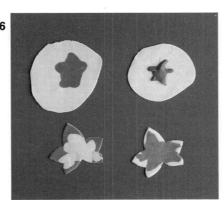

MARBLE CAKE

INGREDIENTS
20cm (8in) square fruit cake
boiled, sieved apricot jam (jelly)
900g (2lb) marzipan
900g (2lb) sugarpaste
green food colouring
icing sugar (confectioner's sugar)

DECORATIONS
2 metres (2 yards) light chiffon ribbon
1 metre (1 yards) thin green ribbon
1 metre (1 yard) thin red ribbon
green net
green-coloured royal icing

EQUIPMENT
rolling pin
sharp knife
25cm (10in) cake board
pastry brush

This is a very quick and simple cake to decorate and should be within the scope of most beginners.

Cover the cake with marzipan and centre on the cake board. Knead sugarpaste thoroughly before adding the colour so that when the two colours are added the paste is only kneaded for a short period. Add a little of the dark green paste colour and knead for a few minutes so that the colour remains separate and streaky. When satisfied with the mix, roll out and apply to the cake in the usual way, pinching the paste at the bottom edge for a more decorative finish. If you have not used this method of colouring paste before, it is advisable to practice on a small piece of paste first to enable you to judge how much colour to add and how little kneading is required.

As the pattern on this cake is so subtle, the decoration on the top should be light and airy so that it does not detract from the marbling. A light chiffon ribbon has been used for the rosette. Holly leaves have been cut from green net, using the template on page 11, and outlined in green-coloured royal icing. The leaves have then been allowed to set over a former so that they will dry with some degree of movement in them. Finally, bands of green and red ribbon have been placed towards the base of the cake.

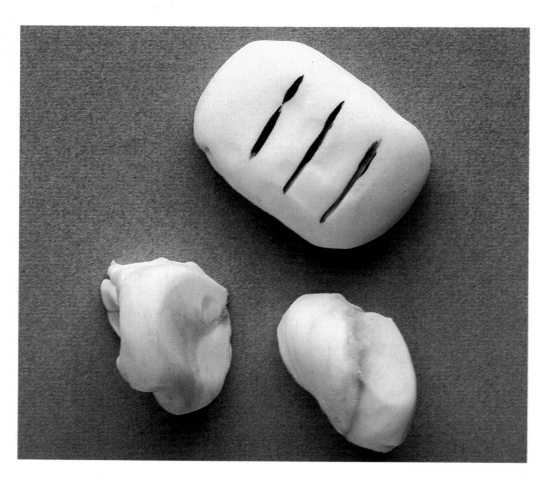

PARCEL CAKE

INGREDIENTS
20cm (8in) round cake
900g (2lb) marzipan
900g (2lb) sugarpaste
blue and red food colouring
silver non-toxic paint
small quantity of white royal icing (optional)

DECORATIONS
3 metres (3 yards) ribbon

EQUIPMENT
25cm (10in) cake board
pastry brush
thin card
scalpel
plastic
greaseproof (waxed) or silicone paper
rolling pin
paintbrush No 0

Ideas for parcel cakes can be obtained by looking at the designs used for Christmas wrapping paper. A shape from one sheet can be used with a shape from another resulting in an original design. Because of the novelty of such a design, it is unlikely that cutters will be available. Templates can be made from thin card; that used for cereal boxes is ideal as it is durable and has a firm edge against which to place the scalpel when cutting. It is essential for the cut edges to be well defined as the overall effect will be spoilt if the shapes are indistinct or damaged. Simplify the design as much as possible as speed is essential. The paste can be kept reasonably moist by covering the entire surface with a plastic sheet.

Cover the cake with marzipan and centre on the board. Prepare the sugarpaste to cover the cake, rolling out to the desired size and shape. Cut out the Christmas trees in various sizes. The trees to be painted silver are better cut from very pale blue paste as this will not effect the colour of the silver when it is applied. Make small balls in red paste and place at random over trees. Lay a sheet of silicone or grease-proof (waxed) paper over the entire area and roll firmly once using the rolling pin. Lay the paste over the cake and finish covering in the usual way.

When the sugarpaste is dry and firm, paint the blue trees silver with a fine brush and non-toxic silver paint. To create the parcel effect, place two pieces of red ribbon across the cake and top with a large ribbon rosette. A band of ribbon is also placed round the cake drum. If desired, a delicate snailstrail may be piped around the base of the cake for an attractive finish.

SCROLL CAKE

INGREDIENTS

20cm (8in) fruit cake
boiled, sieved apricot jam (jelly)
900g (2lb) marzipan
900g (2lb) sugarpaste
50g (2oz) modelling paste
brown and cream dusting powder
sepia brown food colouring
brown paste colour
small quantity royal icing
egg white

DECORATIONS

*holly leaves, berries, Christmas roses and leaves
  (see page 10)*
75cm (30ins) thin gold ribbon
*1 metre (1 yard) gold ribbon the same width as the
  cake drum*

EQUIPMENT

28cm (11in) cake board
small rolling pin
large rolling pin
paper
scissors
ball tool
scalpel
paintbrushes Nos 0, 1
small pieces of foam
cocktail sticks or toothpicks
piece of polythene
pastry brush

Marzipan and cover the cake with white sugarpaste in the normal way. Centre on the cake board.

For the scroll, cut a rectangular piece of paper using the template provided and experiment with the shape by rolling each end until satisfied with the extent the scroll is to be rolled. Be certain to take into consideration the space required for the added foliage. Unwind the paper scroll and use as a template.

Roll out a piece of modelling paste quite finely. Cut and remove small notches from each side. Smooth all cut edges with a large ball tool to thin and curl back some of the tears producing a torn and worn look to the scroll. Roll up the scroll to the same extent as the template above, and support the shape using small pieces of foam and paintbrush handles until dry.

Dust edges with brown- and cream-coloured dusting colour to create the impression of old parchment. Paint lines and notes in a sepia brown colour with a fine brush. Attach to the cake with a small amount of royal icing.

Make holly, berries and Christmas rose as shown on page 10.

PINE CONE

Make two sizes so that the smaller ones can be placed on top of the scroll and the larger at the base to create an illusion of depth.

Make a cone shape in brown paste. Place on a cocktail stick (toothpick) while assembling and remove stick on completion. Roll small balls of paste, flatten between two pieces of polythene. Attach the flattened disc to the cone with egg white and slightly curve back the top edge of each disc. Continue to work down the cone in this way until complete.

Arrange the foliage and flowers around the scroll. Attach ribbons to cake board and base of cake to tone with the colours of the leaves.

scroll template

SNOWMAN

INGREDIENTS

15cm (6in) fruit cake
boiled, sieved apricot jam (jelly)
550g (1¼lb) marzipan
550g (1¼lb) sugarpaste
orange, brown, yellow and brown paste colour
rock crystal sugar
small quantity royal icing
gum arabic glue (optional)

EQUIPMENT

22cm (9in) cake board
rolling pin
sharp knife or scalpel
palette knife
ball tool
fine scissors
modelling tools
pastry brush

Cut a 15cm/6in cake into sections following the instructions as shown.

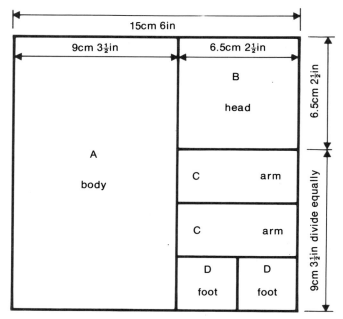

BODY

Round the top edge for the chest. Carve a channel between the legs to separate them and finally, round-off the edges to form the shoulders.
Carve section B into a round ball for the head. Cut section C in half, round-off the edges for arms. Round the edge of both D sections for the feet.

ASSEMBLY

Place arms on each side of the body with marzipan softened with warm apricot jam (jelly) so that it forms a sticky glue. Butt the feet to the base of the legs and position the head. Fill in any holes with marzipan as shown. Cover the assembled cake with marzipan and then with sugarpaste following the normal procedure.

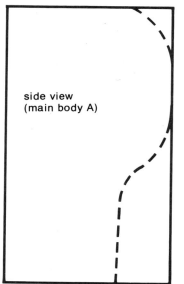

side view
(main body A)

   While the sugarpaste is still soft, insert small pieces of rock sugar for the eyes and mouth. For the nose, make a thin, elongated cone of orange sugarpaste and intent small rings around the resulting carrot-shaped nose using a palette knife or the back of a scalpel. Make a hole in the face and place the carrot in position bending the nose upwards slightly to create an interesting expression. Insert pieces of rock sugar into the body to represent buttons.

HAT

Make a ball of paste. Roll into a thick, short sausage-shape. Pinch out the bottom as in the Mexican hat method of making flowers. Keep pinching and twisting until the brim is the desired size and thickness. Shape the crown by inserting a thumb or ball tool to create a concave shape. The hat should look quite floppy, to give a beguiling air to the snowman.

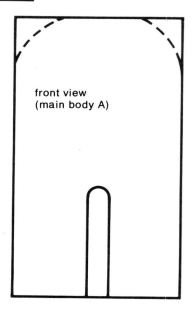

front view
(main body A)

SCARF

Colour some modelling paste yellow. Roll into a long narrow strip. Place paste between a folded new dishcloth. Press firmly all over to imprint the woven pattern onto the paste. Fringe both ends of the scarf with a pair of fine scissors. Wrap around the snowman's neck. Pinch where the knot is to be placed.

KNOT

Make a ball with yellow paste and flatten. Create the knitted look as above then form the creases and folds using a modelling tool. Place on the pinched area at the neck edge.

BESOM (BRUSH)

Using brown modelling paste, roll a long thin sausage, about the size of a pencil; leave to dry. Make a large cone, flatten both ends. Make a hole at the top of the flattened cone large enough for the sausage-shape to be placed inside when both are dry. Cut into the side of the base cone to create twigs. Roll some fine strands and attach all around the cone. Place the dried handle inside the base cone and glue in place with royal icing or gum arabic glue. Secure a small gap at the base of the handle and above this gap, attach a row of narrow strands. Roll a long strand of paste and wrap around the handle in the gap that has been left.

FINISHING

Cover the base board with royal icing to simulate snow. Place the brush in place, attach to the body.

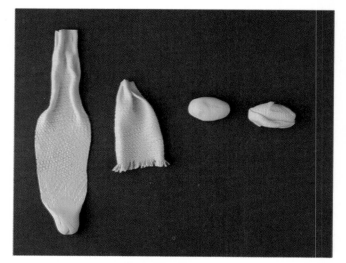

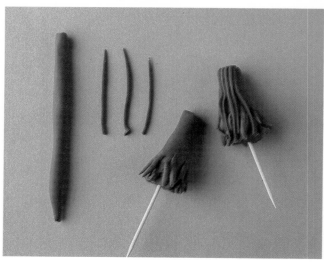

INGREDIENTS

20cm (8in) round fruit cake
boiled, sieved apricot jam (jelly)
900g (2lb) marzipan
900g (2lb) sugarpaste
25g (1 oz) modelling paste
black, white and snowflake dusting powder
medium brown paste colour
cream, red and opaque white paste colour
½ cup royal icing

DECORATIONS

ivy leaves (see page 10)
tay berries and leaves (see page 10)

EQUIPMENT

25cm (10in) cake drum
piece of paper
scissors
rolling pin
paintbrush No 0
tracing paper
scriber
modelling tool
palette knife
pastry brush

Cut a paper template for the moon and hold in place while applying the clouds. These are applied with powder colours in various tones of grey (made by mixing black and white powder colours) which are dusted over the surface of the cake. Use the powder colour sparingly and make sure to knock the excess powder from the brush before applying to the cake.

Start with the paler tones and gradually increase in depth. Remove the paper template. The circle should be quite clean and free from powder. To break up the circular shape slightly, one or two of the cloud shapes can be continued across the moon.

Paint on the branches of the bush in a medium brown tone paste colour. Darken the tone for the thicker branches, again to give a feeling of depth to the picture.

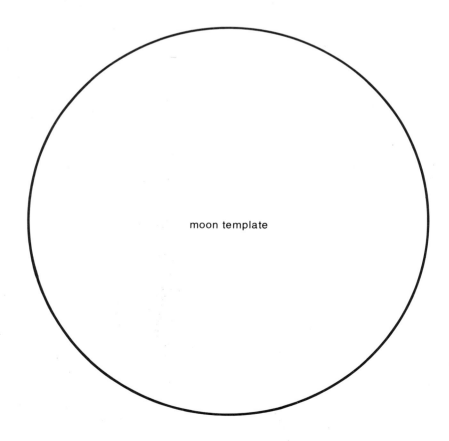

moon template

ROBIN

Trace the outline of the robin onto a piece of tracing paper. Lay the paper on the cake and using a scriber, either prick through the paper to transfer the design, or indent a continuous line to create the image. Using the tracing paper as a guide, take a small piece of sugarpaste and flatten and mould into the shape of the bird. Remove from the paper using a palette knife and transfer to the cake surface. Indent the eye socket and form the shape of the wing with a modelling tool. More paste can be added to the breast area to emphasize.

Using brown modelling paste, roll out two tail feather shapes as shown, and attach one on top of the other. Roll out a piece of white modelling paste slightly larger than the outline of the robin. Lay over the robin and gently stretch and curve over the sugarpaste moulded shape, using the tips of the fingers. Carefully press into the indented areas. Make sure that all edges surrounding the robin are curved under the body shape so that the sugarpaste is completely hidden.

Allow to dry for 24 hours. Paint in the details using paste colour and a fine brush as shown.

Roll two pieces of brown modelling paste quite finely for the legs. Make a small hole into the body of the robin with a scriber and when the legs are dry, insert into the holes. Place the ends of the legs where the feet should be, into a piece of sugarpaste.

FINISHING

Make ivy leaves and tay berry leaves following the instructions for leaves on page 10. Place foliage into the sugarpaste around the feet, it is most important that the wires are not inserted directly into the cake but into the sugarpaste pieces. When the arrangement of the foliage has been completed, apply royal icing to the sugarpaste pieces at the base of the robin to hide the entry of the wires and to simulate snow. This can then be dusted with snowflake sparkle dusting colour when the icing is dry which will produce the illusion of night-time sheen on the snow.

Mix a very pale creamy colour for the stars and paint onto the sky area using a fine brush. Paint an ivy garland at the edge of the cake board as shown.

robin template

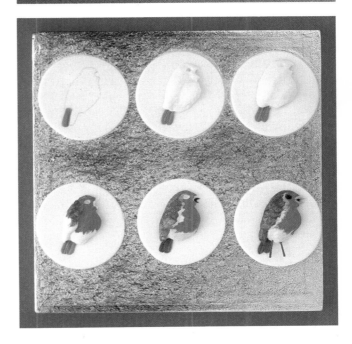

CHRISTMAS PUDDING CAKE

INGREDIENTS

1 spherical fruit cake 15cm (6in) diameter
boiled, sieved apricot jam (jelly)
550g (1¼lb) marzipan
550g (1¼lb) brown-coloured sugarpaste
450g (1lb) custard-coloured sugarpaste
mid brown, dark brown, very dark brown, cream,
*   yellow, pink and black paste colour*
assorted paste colours for painting clothing detail
small quantity royal icing
gum arabic glue

DECORATIONS

2 large holly leaves and 3 berries (see page 10)

EQUIPMENT

spherical cake mould
oval cake board 20 × 25cm (8 × 10in)
scalpel or sharp knife
posy pick
rolling pin
ball tool
paintbrushes Nos 00 and 1
modelling tool
scissors
small pieces of foam
pastry brush

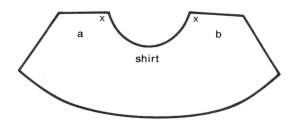

a,b, shirt front edge
x, collar point

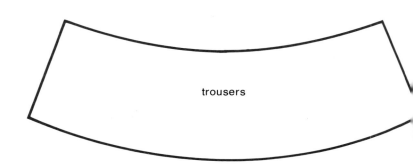

Use a special cake tin (pan) for making a small ball-shape. Carve a small hole at the base of the cake. Wrap the cake with marzipan easing out the fullness. Ease the marzipan into the hole that has been carved. Cut away the excess marzipan at the base of the ball and mask any folds by smoothing gently with the hand. The warmth of the hand should eradicate these fold lines.

Colour some sugarpaste to the colour of fruitcake, use to wrap over the cake as for marzipan. Colour some sugarpaste to a creamy, yellow colour for the custard. Roll out, and using the template, cut out the custard-shape. Place on top of the cake, smoothing out the cut edges to give a rounded effect to the custard. Make two large holly leaves using the instructions on page 10. As the wires must not be placed directly into the cake, insert a posy pick into the top of the cake to hold the wires. The currants on the cake are produced by scratching and picking at the surface of the brown sugarpaste to create irregular shapes. Paint raised shapes a darker brown colour.

MICE
Head

Make a small cone in medium brown-coloured paste. Indent eyes, nostrils and a tiny mouth. For the ears, press a ball of pink-coloured paste between the fingers to flatten. Thin and cup with a ball tool. Pinch the base of the ear together and attach to the head. Texture the surface of the paste with a scalpel making small cuts and scratches. Roll two tiny balls of black-coloured paste and place into the eye sockets. Place a minute piece of pink paste onto the nose and shape with a modelling tool indenting again the nostril area. Make a rounded squat cone-shape and exaggerate the flatness of the body; dress by wrapping in the coloured paste. Use the template provided for the shirt and cut out in yellow sugarpaste. Attach to the upper part of the body, fold back the collar. Cut a rectangular shape for the trousers and wrap the bottom half of the body in this paste ensuring that the seam is at the back of the mouse. When dry, paint any patterns, plaids and stripes onto the clothing.

Feet and Arms

For the arms, take a small piece of pink paste, roll into a sausage shape. Flatten out one end into a thin spade-shape. Cut four long fingers using a fine pair of scissors. Place on foam and indent with a ball tool to curve the fingers. Encase the upper part of the arm in the same colour paste as the shirt. Trim off the excess paste on the inside of the arm and, when dry, attach to the body with royal icing.

Make the feet in the same way as the arms but after indenting the toes with the ball tool, bend to form a foot. When dry, attach to the body. Make a long, thin, tapering tail by rolling pink paste finely and glue into position using gum arabic glue.

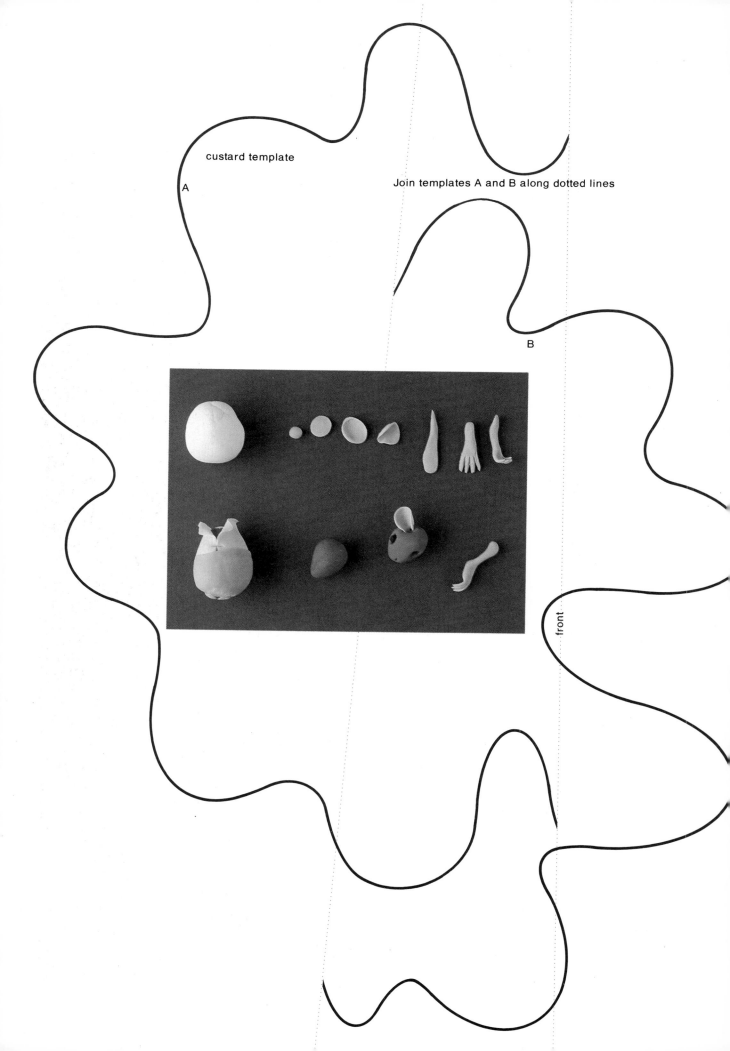

custard template

A

Join templates A and B along dotted lines

B

front

INGREDIENTS

1 Madeira cake 20 × 25cm (8 × 10in)
boiled sieved apricot jam (jelly)
900g (2lb) sugarpaste
dark blue, chestnut, red, flesh-coloured, yellow,
*   licorice and opaque white paste colouring*
small quantity royal icing
blue food colouring
assorted bright paste colours for parcels

DECORATIONS

2 holly leaves (see page 10)
small pieces of coloured ribbons
rosettes and bows for parcels

EQUIPMENT

25cm (10in) square cake board
greaseproof (waxed) paper
Paper for template
rolling pin
sharp knife
ball tool
garlic press or clay gun
black food pen
pastry brush
scalpel or ribbon insertion tool
No3 piping tube

PREPARATION OF CAKE BOARD

Colour some sugarpaste a dark blue colour and roll out to a square just larger than the board. Colour a small amount of paste yellow and cut out small stars in varying sizes. Place the stars on the blue paste as shown, cover with a piece of greaseproof (waxed) paper and roll once to form a single sheet of paste. Use to cover all but the bottom 2.5cm (1in) of the cake board. Cover this bottom strip with chestnut-coloured paste, indent with the knife to form tiles.

CAKE

Turn the baked cake upside-down so that the base is uppermost, trimming off the upper crust if the cake is not level. Cut around the Father Christmas template and cover the cake with marzipan. Cover the cake with red-coloured sugarpaste to the top of the boots.

Cover the boots with black sugarpaste. Indent a line using the back of a knife to separate the boots. Place the covered cake on the prepared board. Cut the soles from chestnut-coloured paste and attach to the boots.

Colour a small piece of paste to a skin colour. Cut out the face shape using the template; attach to the cake. Make a template of the beard and hat trim and cut from white sugarpaste. Place in position over the face. Indent the eye sockets using a small ball tool. Make the mouth by rolling out a small sausage in flesh-coloured paste. Attach to the mouth area.

Make the parcels using the same principle as used for the cake board. Roll the paste to 6mm ($\frac{1}{4}$in) thick, lay over the stripes or dots and roll once to secure. Cut out the parcel shapes using the templates provided and secure in position on the cake.

Model the arm from a piece of red sugarpaste as shown, indenting the cuff area so that the mitt will fit inside. Model the mitt and place inside the cuff and over the parcels.

Roll a ball of red sugarpaste for the nose and flatten slightly, position on the cake. Make the beard by pushing white sugarpaste through a garlic press or clay gun. Attach to the beard area allowing space for the lips to show through. Use a little of the same paste for the eyebrows.

Make a label using the template. Cut two shapes, the larger one in yellow. Place the smaller, white shape on top of the yellow piece and leave to dry flat. When dry, apply the lettering using a black food pen or, with a steady hand, with a brush and licorice paste colour. Make two glazed holly leaves and berries. Attach ribbons to the parcels using the ribbon insertion method. Make a small slit in the sugarpaste at the edge of the parcel and insert in the ribbon edge using a scalpel or ribbon insertion tool. Allow the ribbon to drape over the parcel and secure the other end in the same way. Add a rosette or bow.

Using a large No3 tube, pipe white royal icing onto the fur trim area around the face. Create texture by moving the tube in a circular motion. Make two small balls in white paste and fit into the eye sockets. When dry, paint in the eyes. Add a white highlight using opaque white to bring the eyes to life. Attach the leaves and the label in position.

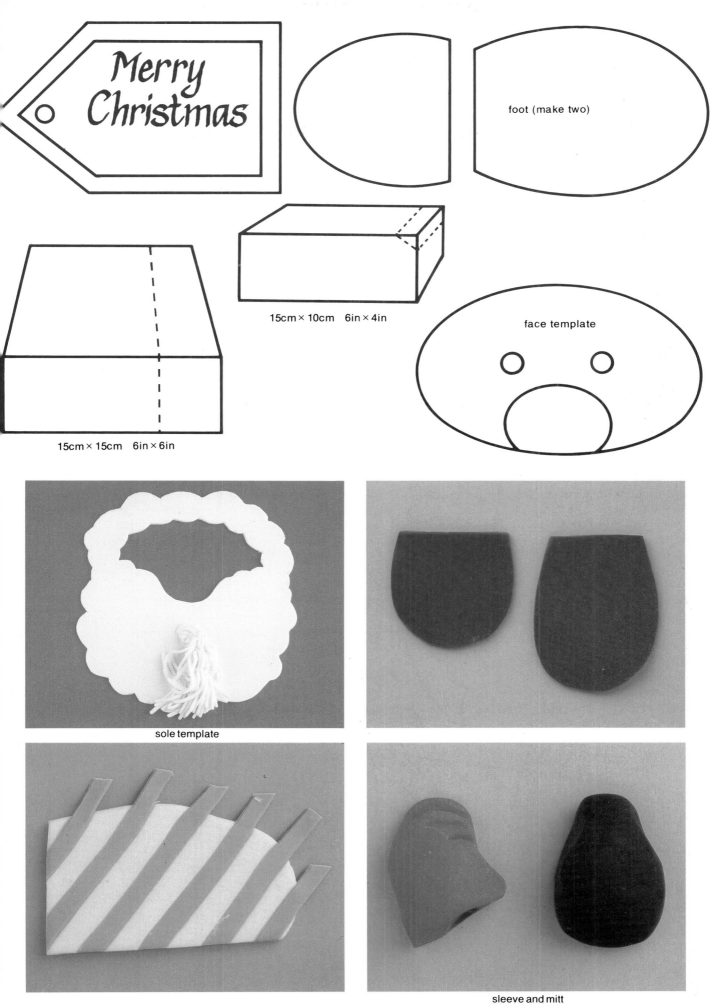

Merry Christmas

foot (make two)

15cm × 10cm   6in × 4in

15cm × 15cm   6in × 6in

face template

sole template

sleeve and mitt

29

Join templates along dotted line
to create whole figure

Merry Christmas

SACK CAKE

INGREDIENTS

1 15cm (6in) square fruit cake, approx. 8cm (3in)
    deep
675g (1½lb) marzipan
550g (1¼lb) sugarpaste
boiled, sieved apricot jam (jelly)
dark brown paste colour or dusting powder
selection of bright paste colours for painting
    parcels and toys

DECORATIONS

bows for parcels

EQUIPMENT

25cm (10in) cake board
pastry brush
rolling pin
sharp knife
modelling tool
dish cloth
thin card

To form the sack shape, cut 5cm (2in) from one side of
the cake leaving a rectangle 10 × 15cm (4 × 6in). Cut
the bottom edge at an angle as shown. Hollow out the
uppermost side of the sack to form the interior of the
sack, you will need to exaggerate the depth of this
hollow as the depth and size will decrease when the
marzipan and sugarpaste are placed on the cake.

Place the cake on a board and anchor well with
marzipan softened with warm apricot jam (jelly). The
slice of cake cut away from the bottom edge can be
placed under the front edge of the cake to help fill up
the gap as shown. Secure in position with marzipan.

Cover the entire sack shape with marzipan. When
covered and while the marzipan is still soft and easy to
mould, exaggerate and pad out the corners of the
sack, also create lumps and bumps to represent the
toys pushing against the sacking. With a modelling
tool, create creases and folds.

Colour the sugarpaste brown and cover the sack.
Take care to pinch and mould the top of the sack to
produce a natural effect. Use a course, clean dishcloth
or a piece of hessian to texture the surface of the
sugarpaste. Allow to dry.

Make a stencil of the word 'TOYS' and either paint
in the letters with paste colour and a paintbrush or use
dark brown dusting colour.

Make toys and parcels to fill in the sack. Beginners
could make a simpler, but attractive cake using
parcels only. Make a feature of the different patterned
wrapping papers and use a selection of coloured
ribbons and bows.

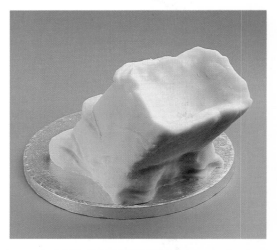

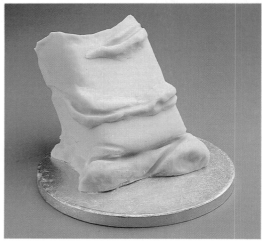

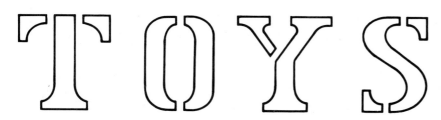

INGREDIENTS

Fruit cake baked in a 15cm (6in) hexagonal tin (pan)
boiled, sieved apricot jam
550g/1¼lb marzipan
550g/1¼lb sugarpaste
yellow, orange, green, red, black, brown and blue food colouring
silver non-toxic paint
gum arabic
modelling paste
skintone and silver dusting powder
colourless spirit (to mix with dusting colours)
small quantity of royal icing
gum arabic

DECORATIONS

Holly leaves and berries (see page 10)
Garrett frill (see page 9)

EQUIPMENT

25cm (10in) cake board
flouncing tool or cocktail stick
paintbrushes Nos 00, 1
Vegetable parchment piping bags
glue brush
large rolling pin
small rolling pin
pastry brush
No 1 and 2 piping tubes
scalpel or sharp knife

Cover the cake in marzipan and sugarpaste following the normal procedure. Scribe the shape of the angel and bauble onto the top of the cake. Draw the basic outline of the angel onto a piece of tracing paper. Use sugarpaste to mould the shape of the body and head inside the drawn outline. Indent where the upper arm and thigh will rest, then indent the eye socket. Exaggerate the indentations as these areas will become smaller when covered with another layer of sugarpaste.

When satisfied with the shape, transfer to the cake using a cranked palette knife. Draw the outline of the front of the face, this need not cover the entire head, as part of it will be covered with hair. Colour some paste to a skintone (paprika with just a touch of melon works well). Place the forehead, nose and mouth edge onto the surface of the cake and, using a finger and

ball tool, gently smooth into the indented and shaped areas making sure that the edge is completely attached to the cake surface and there are no gaps and the sugarpaste is completely covered.

Make the left arm in quite shallow relief and place in position. Make a hand by forming a small, spade shape, and with a pair of scissors, cut out a small V-shape for the thumb. Make four further cuts in the shape that is left. Pull each finger using the same technique as for pulled flowers. Round off each finger tip. Place a ball tool on the hand at the tip of the fingers and stroke towards the palm to curve the fingers. Twist the hand at an angle so that it takes on a natural, sideways position. Repeat for the second hand as far as curling the fingers. Rotate the paste between the fingers and thumb so that a wrist is formed, continue the rolling action to form the elbow and upper arm. Place in a natural position and allow to dry.

Make the leg and the foot in a similar fashion as for the arms. Make a fatter sausage shape, flatten the end for the foot and mark in the toes as for the fingers. Form a heel and an ankle, then make a knee as for the elbow. Finally twist the foot upwards. Allow to dry.

Make a small frill and wrap around the neck and left wrist. Wrap the right arm completely in thin, white paste, cut off the excess paste at the stem edge of the underside so that it will fit into the pre-formed indentation. Add the wrist frill. Place the leg in the indentation and secure with royal icing. Roll out some sugarpaste for the dress and cut out using the template. Secure the arms and the dress in position with royal icing taking care to arrange the folds naturally. Make another frill for the hem of the dress.

Cut out the wings. Thin the cut edges using a ball tool and place one of the wings over a piece of foam to shape and give movement; allow to dry. The other wing should be dried flat with just a little movement in the upper feathers. When the wings are dry, paint the feathers and pipe on small dots with white royal icing to create depth as well as for decoration. Match the wings to the angel. Lay the back wing on the cake surface, but insert the front wing into a pre-carved small hole. Pipe some royal icing into the hole and underneath the wing. Support with foam until dry.

Pipe the hair directly onto the head using golden-coloured royal icing. Brush over with a fine stiff brush to create a rough texture. Paint on the features. Colour the cheeks with a pale skin-tone dusting

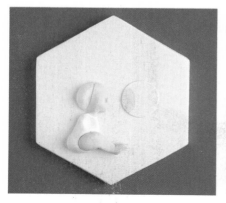
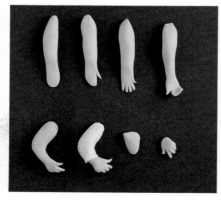

lower arm

face (skin)

dress

sleeve

indent

indent

colour (reduce the colour by adding a little cornflour (cornstarch) and mixing well). Add the holly leaves and berries to the hem and sleeve of the dress.

BAUBLE

Cut out a thin circle of paste for the interior of the bauble. When dry, paint the area that will be cut away, blue. Make a small cone for Father Christmas' hat, tilt slightly sideways at the top of the cone. Make a flattened cone-shape for the body. Paint on the black boots, belt and buttons. When dry, paint on the fur with white royal icing.

Make a large ball-shape as shown with sugarpaste, flatten onto a smooth surface until it fits the size of the template. Cut away the hollow with a scalpel. Carve away the area inside the hollow to give a curved look. Smooth the cut area with fingers and glue into position on the cake. Make a small square for the neck of the bauble and attach, smoothing away the seamline with a modelling tool. Place a slightly larger and thicker square over the neck and create grooves with the back of the scalpel.

Make a ring by rolling a fine strand of paste, make a loop and attach to the top of the bauble. Mix together silver snowflake dusting powder and clear spirit (gin or vodka) to make a paint and use to paint over the bauble to give it a sheen. For the additional raised pattern, paint the band and dots with either gum arabic or egg white. Sprinkle with snowflake sugartex over the glued areas while still wet, remove excess sugartex by tilting the cake. Paint the ring and top silver with non-toxic paint. Pipe in the tree with green and brown royal icing. Attach string to the bauble by rolling a fine strand of paste and looping through the ring onto the tree. Attach the Garrett frill and add holly and berries to correspond with the holly on the angel's dress.

SAINT NICOLAS BAS RELIEF

INGREDIENTS
20cm (8in) oval fruit cake
boiled, sieved apricot jam
900g (2lb) marzipan
450g (1lb) white sugarpaste
675g (1½lb) blueberry blue-coloured sugarpaste
675g (1½lb) modelling paste
*dark blue, flesh-coloured, red, black, mint green
 and brown paste colouring*
non-toxic gold colouring
small quantity royal icing
gum arabic

DECORATION
1 metre (1 yard) blue velvet ribbon

EQUIPMENT
30cm (12in) oval cake board
pastry brush
large rolling pin
small rolling pin
scalpel or sharp knife
vegetable parchment piping bags
No1 piping tube
metal tea strainer
clay gun
glue brush
paintbrushes Nos 00, 1
modelling tools
small pieces of foam
tracing paper
silicone paper
scriber
cocktail stick or toothpick

This cake should only be attempted by experienced cake decorators.

Roll out the dark blue sugarpaste along with a smaller quantity of the white sugarpaste. Slightly thin one edge of both pieces and place the blue edge over the white edge. Roll together making sure that the joined edge is quite smooth; the overall paste should be of the same thickness and be handled as one piece.

Place over the marzipanned cake and board making sure that the sky line is placed in the right position. Continue to cover the cake in the usual way.

Draw the outline of the figure onto a piece of silicone paper. Keeping within the outline, gradually build up the body using sugarpaste. Make depressions where the arm, neck and sack are to be placed. On the face, make a smaller depression for the eye socket.

Transfer the figure carefully onto the cake using a palette knife. Cover the top of the head with a small cap shape for the hat. Cover the right arm with a small piece of red paste. Make sure the edge of the modelling paste is sealed to the cake surface with a modelling tool to give a smooth finish. Roll out a small piece of skin-coloured paste and place over the face. Smooth into the indentations. The eye socket and other facial details should be made as for the angel on page 33. Use a small piece of black paste to cover the shoe shapes. Using the template provided, cut out the coat in red modelling paste. The coat is larger than the drawn outline of the figure to allow for the added body paste. Moisten and drape over the sugarpaste figure. Then use a modelling tool to carefully mould the paste around the body and to shape the folds and creases. Round the cut edge so that the clothes appear to continue all way around the figure.

Roll out some brown paste and cut out the inside and back part of the sack. Glue in position. Make the top part of the sack by drawing the shape onto silicone paper as for the main figure. Keep the paste fairly thick at the base of the sack.

Use a small rolling pin and gradually thin the sack towards the top edge. Cut out the shape of this top edge using the template. Thin the edge with the fingers and fold back to create a natural effect. Glue in place on the figure.

Using red modelling paste, roll out the furled back coat shape using the template provided. Glue in place and support with foam until dry. Cut out the gown front panel. Glue to the coat side edge and roll paste over the touch finished coat shape. This will give quite a rounded three-dimensional effect to the figure.

squirrel on hand

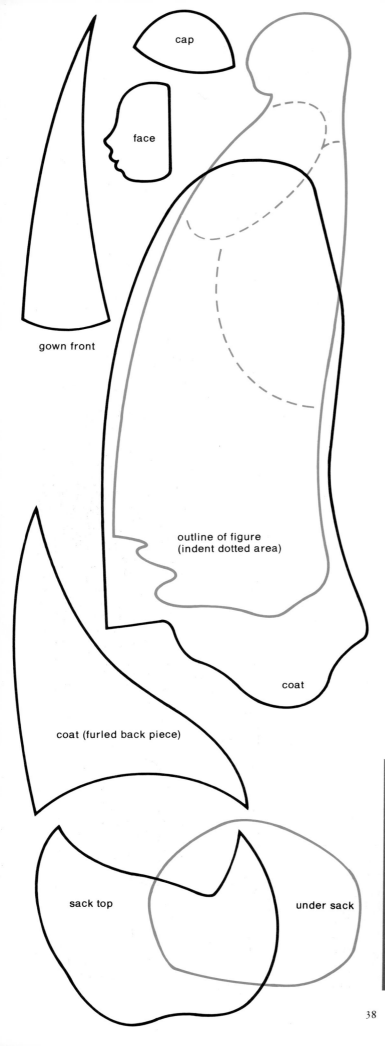

cap

face

gown front

outline of figure
(indent dotted area)

coat

coat (furled back piece)

sack top

under sack

Make the arm from red paste as shown and attach in position with glue.

The hands are fairly basic shapes because of their sideways position. Make a fairly thick, narrow strip in black paste and bend into position as shown. Flatten out the wrist area and glue in position. For the left hand, make a flat, square shape. Make a hole where the base of the thumb should be with a modelling tool. The strap for the sack can be pushed into this hole so that the figure appears to be holding the strap.

The squirrel is made from small pieces of brown and white paste, as illustrated. The tail is piped on at the same time as the figure's beard.

Apply the beard and hair by forcing modelling paste through a clay gun as explained in detail for the Father Christmas in a Chimney cake on page 39. Make the fur for the collar, cuffs and gown edge by pushing sugarpaste through a metal tea strainer to give a soft, textured effect. This will be much softer than the strands created when using a clay gun.

Measure the circumference of the cake, cut out a strip of tracing paper the same length. Fold the paper equally into five sections. Cut a deep scallop out of the top edge of the folded strip. Open the strip and attach all around the cake. Mark the five scallops into the cake surface using a scriber.

Roll out some mint-green-coloured paste. Cut into five long, thin strips. Twist the strip and glue each end into position at the top of each scallop. Cut off any excess paste.

Make bells by rolling small balls of paste each about the size of a seedless grape. Make two cuts in the top of the ball using a sharp knife. At each end of the cuts, indent a small hole with a tiny ball tool or a glass-headed pin. When dry, paint the bells gold using a non-toxic paint. Make a small hole above the twisted green paste with a cocktail stick or toothpick. Roll a fine strand of paste and insert into the hole; loop it over the twisted strips and glue to the cake side directly under the strips. Attach the gold balls with royal icing under the loops. Paint the loops gold when dry.

Pipe in the trees with brown royal icing and a No1 tube. When dry, pipe snow onto the branches using white royal icing. Place velvet ribbon around the cake board to trim.

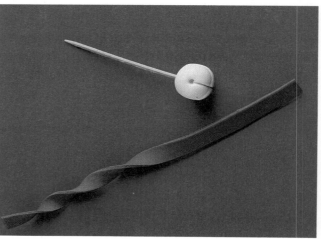

INGREDIENTS

20cm (8in) oval fruit cake
boiled, sieved apricot jam (jelly)
900g (2lb) marzipan
1.8kg (4lb) sugarpaste
125g (5oz) modelling or gelatine paste
paprika, skintone, red, black, blue, white and
  brown paste colours
assorted food colourings for parcels
gold non-toxic food colouring
gum arabic
small quantity royal icing

EQUIPMENT

30cm (12in) oval cake board
pastry brush
small rolling pin
large rolling pin
scalpel or sharp knife
vegetable parchment piping bags
piping tube No1
metal tea strainer
clay gun
glue brush
paintbrushes Nos 0000, 1
modelling tools
tracing paper
cocktail sticks or dowelling
clean dishcloth

Colour half of the sugarpaste to a brick colour using paprika colouring and use to cover the cake. Deepen the shade of some of the remaining paste using additional paprika. Cut out rectangles in the deeper colour to represent the bricks and place around the cake as shown, covering roughly two-thirds of the sides. Make a template for the snow overhang by drawing round the board base and drawing in the snow pattern. Roll out the white sugarpaste, cut around the template with a scalpel and smooth the cut edges so they become rounded. Place over the cake.

FATHER CHRISTMAS AND CHIMNEY

Make a round cone shape for the body. Tilt it slightly backwards so that it appears to be quite rounded. Flatten the top to create shoulders. Make a depression each side of the cone below the shoulders where the arms are to be placed. Allow to dry.

  Make the chimney by forming a large square in

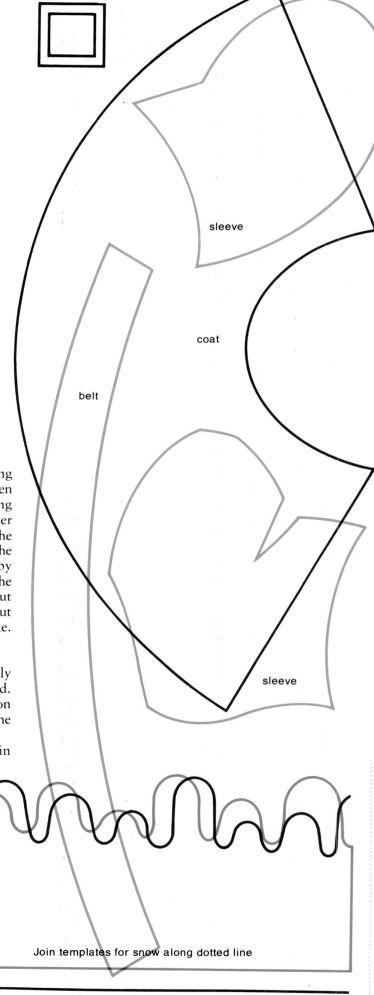

snow on chimney template   Join templates for snow along dotted line

modelling or gelatine paste. Make a hollow in the centre of the square large enough to accommodate the cone-shaped body of the Father Christmas. Try to keep the sides of the chimney fairly square while forming the hollow. Allow to dry. When dry, cover the chimney in the same base colour sugarpaste as used for the cake sides, then add bricks as before. Place in position with royal icing on top of the cake.

Head

Face and head moulds can be made by pushing the head of a doll onto a piece of gelatine or modelling paste and allowing this to dry. The head of Father Christmas has been made by using such a mould. Form a ball of skin-coloured paste, slightly larger than the face area in the mould. Dust the mould with cornflour (cornstarch) so that the face will come away cleanly. It does not matter if the back of the head has pinched fingermarks as these will be covered with the hair, but try to keep the shape as round as possible. Cut away any paste that has formed at the sides of the face and smooth into shape. Place on a cocktail stick or piece of dowelling so that it can dry. Before making the arms, place the cone body inside the chimney so that the position and length of the arms can be checked and made to look natural when holding the chimney and the sack.

Arms

Model the arms by rolling white paste to form a sausage shape. Create a point at one end on which the hand will be attached. Flatten out the paste at the base of the point to form the cuff of the sleeve, bend the sausage to form an elbow and pinch the elbow point to shape it. Place the arm on the cone body to ensure the length and position is correct, pinch off the excess paste. Cut away the inside area of the upper arm so that it will lie snugly against the body and it will fit inside the indentation at the top of the cone; leave to dry. When dry, roll out some red modelling paste and cut out a sleeve shape using the template provided. Wrap around the arm so that the seam is hidden on the underside of the arm. Cut away any excess paste on the inner shoulder area.

Face

Paint in the white of the eyes and exaggerate the wrinkles by painting them in using a paprika or dark skintone colour. When the eyes are dry, paint in the blue iris and the black pupil. Focus the eyes on something so that they do not appear vacant and staring. Use some dusting colour and add a blush to the cheeks and redden the nose. Paint the lips in a darker skintone and darken the inside of the mouth. Roll out some red modelling paste and cut around the coat using the template. Wrap around the cone shape so that the seam edge is in the front. Attach to the head using royal icing.

Hair and Beard

Soften some sugarpaste or modelling paste by adding a little egg white and force through a potter's clay gun. If sugarpaste is used, handle carefully as the consistency is quite soft and fine hair strands can become flattened quite easily. A finer effect can be achieved if modelling paste is used as this becomes quite firm when dry, however, this is far more difficult to use as it takes a great deal of force to push it through the clay gun. Start by applying the strands of hair to the eyebrows, temple and the top of the head. Then begin working at the base of the beard and gradually work upwards towards the chin. Add the hair to the back of the head and finally, add the moustache. While the beard is still soft, attach the arms so that the beard and hair can be arranged over the shoulders.

Hat

Make the hat by forming a cone shape in red paste, flatten out the base with the fingers, turning and thinning the paste until it fits the head. Curve the top of the hat over as in the photograph. Make a small ball from white paste and attach to the end of the cap. Make some small strands using sugarpaste pushed through a clay gun and attach to the ball. Place the hat on the head while the hair is still soft and easily arranged over the edge of the hat.

Belt

Colour some sugarpaste dark brown and roll it out quite thinly. Cut a narrow strip of paste and attach around the waist. Cut out a small square for the belt buckle just slightly wider than the width of the belt. Cut a smaller square from the inner area of the buckle and place on the belt. Paint with non-toxic gold paint when dry. Place the figure in the chimney and secure with royal icing.

Sack

Colour some modelling paste mid-brown. Try to achieve a shape similar to that used to form the Sack Cake on page 31. Shape the sack by forming a large sausage shape. Hollow it out at one end and thin the edge. Pinch out the corners at the base. Create lumps and bumps on the sides of the sack by pushing a ball

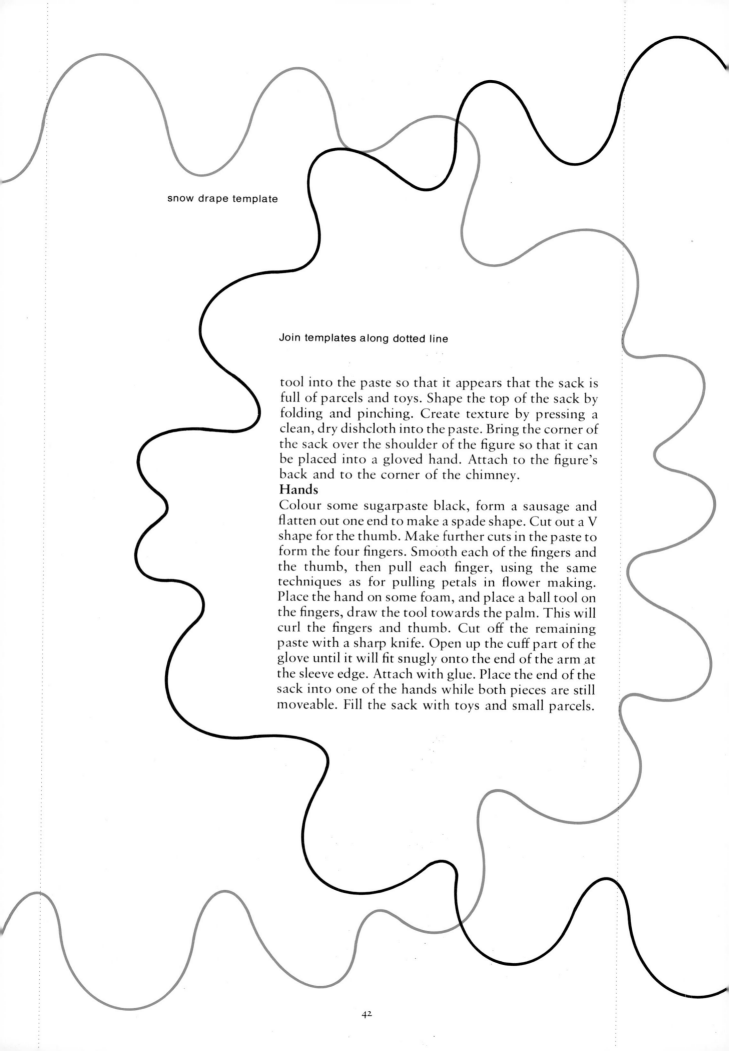

snow drape template

Join templates along dotted line

tool into the paste so that it appears that the sack is full of parcels and toys. Shape the top of the sack by folding and pinching. Create texture by pressing a clean, dry dishcloth into the paste. Bring the corner of the sack over the shoulder of the figure so that it can be placed into a gloved hand. Attach to the figure's back and to the corner of the chimney.

Hands

Colour some sugarpaste black, form a sausage and flatten out one end to make a spade shape. Cut out a V shape for the thumb. Make further cuts in the paste to form the four fingers. Smooth each of the fingers and the thumb, then pull each finger, using the same techniques as for pulling petals in flower making. Place the hand on some foam, and place a ball tool on the fingers, draw the tool towards the palm. This will curl the fingers and thumb. Cut off the remaining paste with a sharp knife. Open up the cuff part of the glove until it will fit snugly onto the end of the arm at the sleeve edge. Attach with glue. Place the end of the sack into one of the hands while both pieces are still moveable. Fill the sack with toys and small parcels.

PAINTED RABBIT

INGREDIENTS

20cm (8in) oval fruit cake
boiled, sieved apricot jam (jelly)
900g (2lb) marzipan
900g (2lb) sugarpaste
modelling paste
assorted food colourings
orange sparkle, and glitter green dusting colour
clear spirit (gin, vodka or kirsch)
small quantity of royal icing (optional)
gum arabic

DECORATIONS

13cm (5in) oval plaque
1 metre (1 yard) thin ribbon

EQUIPMENT

30cm (12in) oval cake board
pastry brush
large rolling pin
small rolling pin
scalpel or sharp knife
glue brush
paintbrushes Nos 000, 0 1
card for templates
tracing paper
13cm (5in) oval plaque cutter
No 1 piping tube

PAINTING ON SUGARPASTE

When painting on sugarpaste, the paste should have been left to dry for at least four days. When working, keep the brush fairly dry, too much moisture will cause streaking and may affect the surface of the paste. If a scene is to be painted, subtle blending of colour can be achieved by brushing one colour into the next while both are still wet. If a pattern or design with clearly defined lines is to be painted, one colour should be completely dry before an adjacent colour or surface pattern is applied. If confident, the painting may be worked directly onto the cake surface, but as mistakes are hard to rectify, you may prefer to paint onto a plaque which can be replaced if the painting does not turn out as expected.

Paste or liquid colours can be used, but avoid the temptation to use colour directly from the pot. Alternatively, you may wish to mix your own colours using dusting colours and a clear spirit (eg. gin, vodka or kirsch) to form a paint. A scene from nature such as that illustrated here used a range of subtle colours and requires a great deal of blending and mixing. This is true of most painted scenes, except maybe if working a particularly bold design or pattern.

PAINTED RABBIT

Immediately the cake has been covered, use an oval biscuit (cookie) or plaque cutter to impress into the cake surface. Remove the cutter carefully and then simply remove the unwanted paste. This results in a sharp-edged inset. If a more rounded effect is required, cover the cake again and carefully drape the paste into the cut-out area, smooth gently with the fingers, then continue to cover as normal.

Cover the cake in the usual way, but where the oval shape is to be cut out, leave the area dry so that the covering layer will not adhere to the base layer. The painting can be worked on the sugarpaste surface, or if preferred, a thin gelatine plaque can be inset into the cut-out shape.

To work the framework surround on top of the surface of the cake, paint in the leaves, ferns and the other ornamentation in pale, subtle colours. When applying the cut-work, increase the strength of the colour so that the painted foliage will move into the background, giving depth to the picture.

For the cut-work design, cutters can be used for some of the leaves, but if an exact size or shape is unavailable, a template should be made from firm, thin card. Cut around the template with a scalpel taking care to give a really clean, sharp edge to the paste. A design, however pleasing, can be completely spoilt by indistinct shapes or damaged lines.

Start on the background shapes first and gradually work forward. For example, to work the pale green leaves surrounding the Christmas tree bauble, cut out the leaves first and arrange on the cake. Cut away the circular shape from the base of the leaves using a tube and place the bauble in the cut out area. Add finishing touches by painting in the veining and shading. Remember when adding detail that the colours will not be true when applied to coloured paste. For example, yellow paint will become green when applied to blue paste. If a lot of the pattern is to be painted, it is therefore better to cut out the shapes using white paste and then paint in the various colours as required.

Finally, add further depth by dusting the holly leaves with a darker shade of green and dust the birds' heads and around the base of their wings with a deeper pink. Take great care when applying the dusting colour directly onto the cake surface. Knock all the excess dust off the brush, otherwise, this could settle onto the white sugarpaste which would completely ruin the effect and make the cake look dirty. Trim the cake with a band of ribbon and pipe a thin snailstrail at the base of the cake, if desired.

rabbit template

DRAPED CAKE WITH CHRISTMAS ROSES

INGREDIENTS
20cm (8in) round fruit cake
boiled, sieved apricot jam (jelly)
900g (2lb) marzipan
900g (2lb) sugarpaste
small amount royal icing
gum tragacanth

DECORATIONS
6 Christmas roses (page 10)
18 ivy leaves (page 10)
1 metre (1 yard) thin cream or gold ribbon

EQUIPMENT
27.5cm (11in) cake board
pastry brush
large rolling pin
vegetable parchment icing bags
No 1 piping tube
tracing paper
tracing wheel or pastry cutter
cocktail stick or toothpick

By using ivy with Christmas roses, the colour scheme for this particular cake is quite different to the usual green and red found when holly and berries are used.

Cover the cake first with marzipan and then with white sugarpaste in the usual way. To make the drape, knead 5ml (1tsp) gum tragacanth into each 450g (1lb) of sugarpaste and leave for 24 hours in a cool place, this will ease handling and ensure that the paste is strong and firm when dry. Use leftover paste for the frills.

Make a paper template larger than the cake board. The drape on the cake shown here is 33cm (13in) in diameter while the board is 27.5cm (11in). The drape is to be lifted at six points, mark these positions on the template. Roll out the sugarpaste until it is almost transparent. That shown here has been placed over striped paper and, as seen, the stripes are clearly visible. Place the template on the paste and cut around it using a tracing wheel or pastry cutter which will create an attractive edge. Mark on the six points where the drape is to be lifted.

It is not necessary to attach the drape to the cake with egg white or water. Simply pick up the paste carefully, supporting with both hands so that it does not stretch out of shape, and place on the cake. Make sure that the same amount of paste is overhanging on all sides of the cake. Where the drape is to be lifted, raise with a cocktail stick or toothpick and, when satisfied with the lay of the folds, push the stick into the cake. When the drape is dry, remove the stick by gently twisting before pulling it out.

Arrange the Christmas roses and ivy leaves into small sprays, rolling the wires up around a pencil and then twisting them out of sight. Attach the entire spray to the drape using royal icing. Apply the ribbon banding in a colour that blend well with the flowers and leaves.

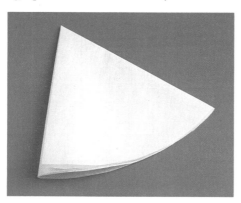

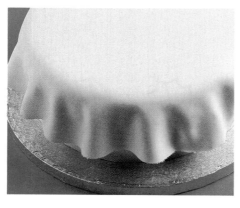

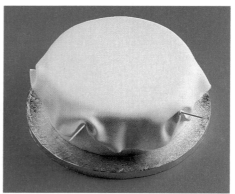

BIRD SCENE COCOA PAINTING

INGREDIENTS

20cm (8in) oval fruit cake
boiled, sieved apricot jam (jelly)
900g (2lb) marzipan
900g (2lb) sugarpaste
cream food colouring
coconut oil or cocoa butter
cocoa powder
small amount royal icing

DECORATIONS

1 metre (1 yard) thin cream ribbon
1.5 metres (1½ yards) thin brown ribbon

EQUIPMENT

30cm (12in) oval cake board
paintbrushes Nos 000, 0, 1, 2
brown food pen or brown lip pencil
vegetable parchment piping bags
large rolling pin
pastry brush

COCOA PAINTING

Cocoa painting is similar in technique to painting with oil paint. Depending on the degree of difficulty of the chosen design, it can be quite a quick and easy way to decorate a cake.

If confident, the design can be painted directly onto

the cake surface, alternatively, the scene may be painted onto a plaque made of sugarpaste, marzipan or gelatine paste. This latter method enables the recipient to keep the plaque as a memento of the occasion.

The outline of the design should not be drawn in too much detail as this will be clearly visible where the tones are light. If sketching the outline, use a brown lip pencil and not an ordinary pencil. However, the ideal method of transferring the design to the cake is to use a scriber.

Traditionally cocoa butter is used but this is difficult to obtain and quite expensive. Coconut oil makes a good substitute, it produces a similar effect and can be easily obtained from good food shops or from health food stores.

To prepare the varying tones of brown colour, put a teaspoon of the coconut oil into each of four pots. Place the pots into a shallow pan of hot water. Add a little cocoa powder to the first container, a little more to the next container and even more to the third. This should result in three distinct tones. In the fourth container make a really dark, concentrated mixture which will be used to define the eyes, deep shadows and lines. During the painting the water will be cooling down so make sure that it is replaced frequently. If the design has to be left before it is completed, seal the pots and store. When ready to use again, return the pots to the hot water and stir well as the cocoa tends to separate from the fat when cold.

CHILDREN WITH BIRDS SCENE

Cover the cake with marzipan and then with cream-coloured sugarpaste as usual. Make an oval plaque approximately 18cm (6in) long and leave for 3–4 days to dry completely.

Cover the area to be worked on in the palest tone of cocoa colour with a large brush. Next paint in the medium tone. Work in the more clearly defined areas, such as the inside of the window, using the darkest of the three tones. Lighten the faces of the two children by removing some of the colour with a dry brush, then add the features and the hands using a very fine brush such as number 0 or 00.

Allow the plaque to dry. When dry, work on the very dark areas by applying the concentrated mixture to the inside of the window, branches of the tree and the lines of the brickwork. Finally, paint on the birds.

When the picture has dried, using a scriber, scratch away some of the colour to create highlights. Add snow to the branches, window panes and sills by piping on white royal icing.

Place the plaque on the cake and trim with a narrow ribbon band. Also apply ribbon banding and bows to the sides of the cake. Keep this fairly simple so as not to detract from the image on the cake surface.

MICE IN WRAPPING PAPER

INGREDIENTS

20cm (8in) round fruit cake
boiled, sieved apricot jam (jelly)
900g (2lb) marzipan
900g (2lb) sugarpaste
modelling paste
assorted food colourings
silver and gold non-toxic paint
opaque white colour
gum arabic

DECORATIONS

ribbon oddments in assorted colours

EQUIPMENT

27.5cm (11in) cake board
pastry brush
large rolling pin
small rolling pin
glue brush
paintbrushes Nos 000, 0, 1
modelling tools
scalpel or sharp knife
small pieces of foam

Cover the cake in marzipan and then in white sugarpaste following the normal procedure.

MICE

Make two heads as shown on page 24. Make another cone shape for the body and attach with royal icing. Make another cone and insert two feet into the base. Make a small hole for the tail. The tail itself will have to be added once the mouse is in position on the cake.

WRAPPING PAPER

Colour some modelling paste a suitable colour for Christmas wrapping paper, for example, red, green or gold. Remember that a pattern will be added at a later stage so it is necessary to keep the shade of the paper fairly pale to enable the design to be clearly visible.

Roll out the paste quite thinly into a roughly square shape, then roll out a second square from a piece of white paste or piece coloured to a paler shade of the initial colour. Place the second piece of paste onto the first piece of paste and roll together firmly to form a single sheet of paste. Cut the paste into a square and ball the edges with a large ball tool so that the edges are thin but not frilled. Experiment by draping, rolling and curling the resulting sheet of paste to form a crumpled look. Place the mouse inside one of the folds. Support the corners and folds, if necessary until dry. Make further pieces of crumpled, coloured paste and arrange on the cake. Add the mouse with tail when the cake is suitably covered. When dry, paint the patterns on the sheets of paper.

Attach ribbons and gift tags as shown and attach the tails to the mice. The board can be covered in short strips of coloured sugarpaste which can be painted when dry to match the cake top.

HOLLY BELL

INGREDIENTS

Fruit cake baked in a 20cm (8in) diameter bell mould
boiled, sieved apricot jam (jelly)
900g (2lb) marzipan
900g (2lb) sugarpaste
100g (4oz/½ cup) green-coloured royal icing
50g (2oz/¼ cup) red-coloured royal icing
gum arabic

DECORATIONS

Holly leaves and berries (see page 10)
2 metres (2 yards) red ribbon

EQUIPMENT

30cm (12in) cake board
pastry brush
large rolling pin
scriber
Garrett frill cutter
tracing paper
No 1 piping tube
vegetable parchment piping bags
glue brush

Place the cake on the cake board and check that the lower edge is nicely rounded as some cake tins are quite flat in this area. If not, then emphasize the curve with a strip of marzipan about 4cm (1½in) wide. Apply the strip so that it runs completely around the base of the bell. Round the top edge of the strip using the palm of the hand until the marzipan strip and cake become one shape. Continue to cover the entire bell in marzipan and white sugarpaste in the usual way.

Use a strip of tracing paper about 5–8cm (2–3in) wide to measure the circumference of the cake. Fold the measured tracing paper into six equal parts. Fold the paper in half again and draw a curve on the paper. Attach the paper around the bell and scribe at the top edge of the pattern. Make the Garrett frills as shown on page 9. Attach the first frill around the base of the bell so that the bottom edge of the frill is near the board. The second frill will then be placed above it onto the scribed line.

Pipe some holly lace using the template provided and green royal icing. Place onto the top edge of the frill securing with royal icing. Pipe red berries between the holly leaves.

Make a decorative spray for the top of the cake using mostly holly and berries. Include red ribbon loops with extended tails to hang against the bell below the spray. Make the hoop with modelling paste and when dry wrap in red ribbon. Position the spray on top of the cake, again securing with royal icing.

repeat to surround cake

52

CHRISTMAS TREE

INGREDIENTS
15 × 20cm (6 × 8in) rectangular Madeira cake
boiled, sieved apricot jam (jelly)
675g (1½lb) marzipan
675g (1½lb) sugarpaste
Christmas green, brown, yellow and red paste
  colouring
gum arabic glue
50g (2oz) flower paste
small quantity royal icing

DECORATIONS
ribbon offcuts approx. 10–12cm (4–5in) in length

EQUIPMENT
24 × 30cm (9½ × 12in) cake board
large rolling pin
small rolling pin
pastry brush
fine scissors
ball tool
small piece fine mesh net
glue brush
tracing paper
card for templates
veiner
small pieces of foam
vegetable parchment piping bag
No 1 piping tube
scalpel

CHRISTMAS TREE CAKE
Using the template provided, cut out the shape of the tree. Cover with marzipan, then cover with sugarpaste coloured with Christmas green paste colouring. Use the template to cut the tub from the leftover cake. Cover with marzipan and then with brown-coloured sugarpaste. Place in position at the base of the tree.

CHRISTMAS ROSE
Use a large blossom cutter that is as close as possible to the size of the rose on the template. Cut out the petals. Use a pair of fine scissors to cut a deeper V between the petals. Ball the edges of each petal and cup each one by placing them onto a piece of foam and gently pressing the ball tool in the centre of each petal. Construct the flowers and place a small ball of yellow paste in the centre of each one. Stretch a piece of fine-meshed net over the centres to add texture. Make 6 to 8 roses.

PARTLY CLOSED ROSES
Make these as suggested above to the cupping stage, then push the lower petals in an upwards position. Support with foam until dry. Place in the yellow centre. Make 2 to 3.

BUDS
Make a small ball, form it into a cone shape and cut in half so that it will lay flat on the tree. Smooth the cut edge. Cut a line on one side of the cone from the top to the base with a scalpel. Lift the edge slightly so that it looks like the edge of a petal. Make about 4 buds.

HOLLY
Make holly leaves and berries following the instructions of page 10.

POINSETTIA
Colour some paste red. Cut the leaves in various sizes using the templates. Indent the veins with a veiner and ball the cut edges. Place the petals in position and secure with gum arabic glue. Make small balls of yellowish green-coloured paste and position in the centre of each flower. The leaves are made in the same way as the petals. Make 2 flowers and a selection of leaves.

ASSEMBLING THE CAKE
Place the flowers and leaves in position using the diagram as a guide. It is wise to make more flowers and leaves than required to provide a choice and to ensure against breakages. Attach to the cake using royal icing. Secure the ribbons to the tub also with royal icing. Pipe a small snailstrail around the base of the cake in green royal icing.

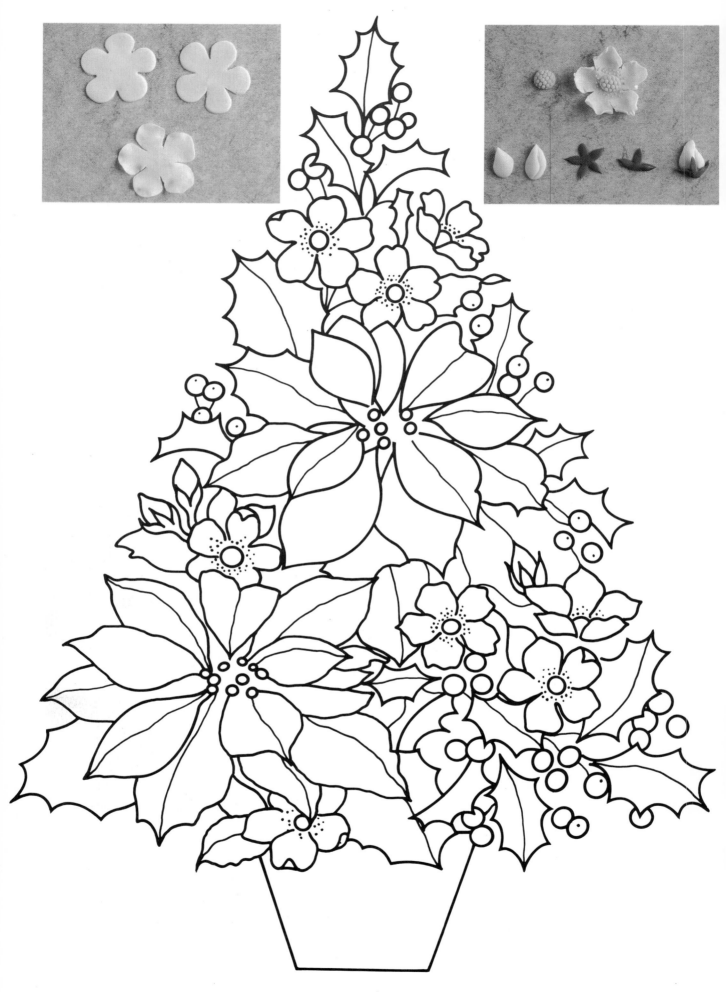

MERRY CHRISTMAS PLAQUE CAKE

INGREDIENTS

20cm (8in) square fruit cake
boiled, sieved apricot jam (jelly)
900g (2lb) marzipan
900g (2lb) sugarpaste
25g (1oz) flower paste
non-toxic gold paint
yellow, red and blue paste colourings
small quantity royal icing
gum arabic glue

DECORATIONS

3 metres (3 yards) thin red ribbon
3 metres (3 yards) thin green ribbon
holly leaves (see page 10)
Christmas roses (see page 10)

EQUIPMENT

27.5cm (11in) cake board
pastry brush
large rolling pin
small rolling pin
scalpel
small star cutter
paintbrushes Nos 00, 1
gelatine plaque, 15cm (6in) oval
vegetable parchment icing bag
tracing paper

Cover the cake with marzipan and white sugarpaste as usual. When the surface is dry and firm, measure the centre point on each of the four sides of the cake and mark at the base. Secure one end of the thin red ribbon at this point with a dot of royal icing. Attach over the top corner and down the next side, attach at the marked point of the second side with royal icing. Continue in this fashion until all four sides have been covered with ribbon. Repeat again using the green ribbon. This ribbon will have to be placed on top of the red ribbon at the centre points, but should be placed alongside the red ribbon at each corner allowing a small gap of about 3mm ($\frac{1}{8}$in) between the two ribbons.

The stars attached to the corners are quite small. To reduce the strain on the eyes and make painting easier, colour the flower paste to a pale yellow for the stars which are to be painted gold, if you were painting the stars silver, colour the paste to a very light blue.

Roll out the yellow paste quite thinly and cut out small stars with a plunger cutter. Using gum arabic glue, attach the stars to the four corner areas created by the ribbons. When dry, paint with gold non-toxic paint.

Scribe the words 'Merry Christmas' onto the plaque using the template and paint in a dark red using a fine brush. Some of the red colours available are quite bright and garish. Burgundy is a much richer colour and can easily be mixed by adding a little blue to the red. When the lettering has been completed, attach the plaque to the centre of the cake using royal icing. Make holly leaves and Christmas roses as shown on page 10. Arrange in place along with three small simple ribbon loops and attach with royal icing.

RIBBON LOOPS

Make four figure-of-eight bows using both red and green ribbon. Holding the red ribbon in your left hand, bring it around your hand so that it lies flat and forms a loop. Repeat again in the opposite direction, but still keeping the ribbon flat so as to form a figure-of-eight. Cut off the ribbon so that the end is longer than the actual loop. Repeat for the remaining ribbon loops. Bind the loops with wire. Lay the wire across the ribbon, then fold the ribbon in half and twist the wire to hold the loops in place. Trim the ends of the ribbon with either an angled or a swallow-tail cut. Cut off the excess wire. Place in position on the board and attach with royal icing.

CAKE WITH COLLAR

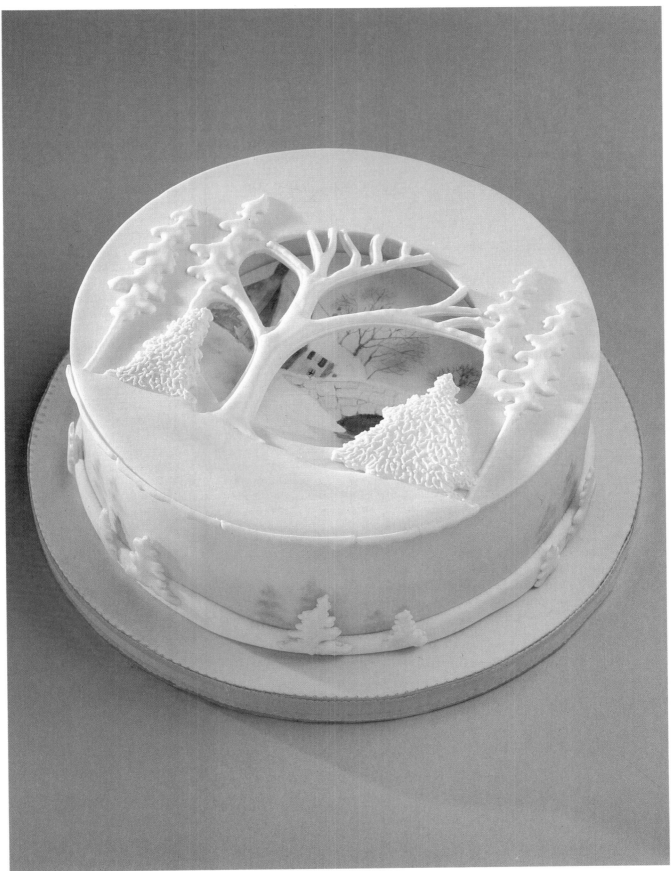

INGREDIENTS

20cm (8in) round fruit cake
boiled, sieved apricot jam (jelly)
900g (2lb) marzipan
1.4kg (3lb) sugarpaste
5ml (1 tsp) gum tragacanth
225g (8oz/1 cup) royal icing
selection of paste colours
lilac, grey and yellow dusting colours
cornflour (cornstarch)

EQUIPMENT

plaque cutter
27.5cm (11in) round cake board
sharp knife
thin 17cm (5½in) round gelatine plaque
pastry brush
paintbrushes Nos 000, 0, 1, 2
thin, firm card
tracing paper
No 1 piping tube
vegetable parchment piping bags
lip pencil
22.5cm (9in) round cake tin (pan)
wax or silicone paper for run-outs

PREPARATION OF CAKE

To make the inset in the cake, turn the cake upside-down and cut a 2.5cm (1in) slice from the surface. Use a plaque cutter and cut a circle approximately 16cm (6½in) in diameter from the slice. Brush the cake with apricot jam (jelly) and replace the ring of cake. Press firmly into place.

COVERING THE CAKE

Spread jam (jelly) on the top of the cake, invert and place the sticky surface onto a rolled out piece of marzipan. Cut round the edge of the cake with a sharp knife. Then, either cut away the centre of the inset using the same-sized plaque cutter, or feel with the fingers to find the edge of the inset, and cut away the middle section of marzipan with a sharp knife.

Measure the depth of the inset. Roll out a long, narrow strip of marzipan. Cut each edge sharply with a knife to this measurement. Roll up the strip carefully, and then unroll while attaching to the side edge of the inset. Butt the ends together and smooth over the join. Measure the base of the inset with a pair

of dividers. Make a template out of card to this measurement and use the template to cut a circle of marzipan. Spread jam (jelly) onto the exposed surface of the cake and attach the inner circle of marzipan. Measure the depth and the circumference of the cake. Roll out a piece of marzipan to these measurements. Cut the edges of the marzipan quite straight using a sharp knife. Cover the side of the cake with jam (jelly) and roll it along the strip of marzipan. Butt the edges together and smooth to hide the join. This method of marzipanning will ensure that all the edges are quite sharp and not rounded.

Cover the cake with sugarpaste in the usual way. Ease gently into the cut-out area, still keeping the edge as sharp as possible. When completed, measure the diameter of the inset and make a template to fit. Cut out a thin gelatine plaque using the template and allow to dry.

COLLAR AND BORDERS

Although collars are traditionally made of royal icing, they can be effective made from sugarpaste. However, gum tragacanth powder must be kneaded into the sugarpaste to give the collar additional strength. Use 450g (1lb) sugarpaste for the collar and knead in 5ml (1 tsp) gum tragacanth powder into the paste. Leave for 24 hours before use.

Roll out the sugarpaste and cut around template A using a scalpel. Leave to dry. When firm enough, carefully turn the collar over and allow the underside to dry.

When the collar is completely dry, pipe the outline of the trees and the foreground using royal icing and template B as a guide. Fill inside the piped outlines with royal icing made to run-out consistency. Work on the trees and areas in the background first, then gradually work forwards. When the run-out work is dry, pipe the surfaces of the fir trees in the foreground with cornelli work to create a three-dimensional effect.

Make a sugarpaste strip following the template and place in position at the base of the cake. For the trees, pipe the outline in royal icing then fill in using run-out consistency royal icing. Leave these runouts to dry on a 22.5cm (9in) round cake tin (pan) so that they will be gently curved and will fit into position on the finished cake. Make the run-out collar border in four sections following the template, allow to dry on the cake tin (pan) as before.

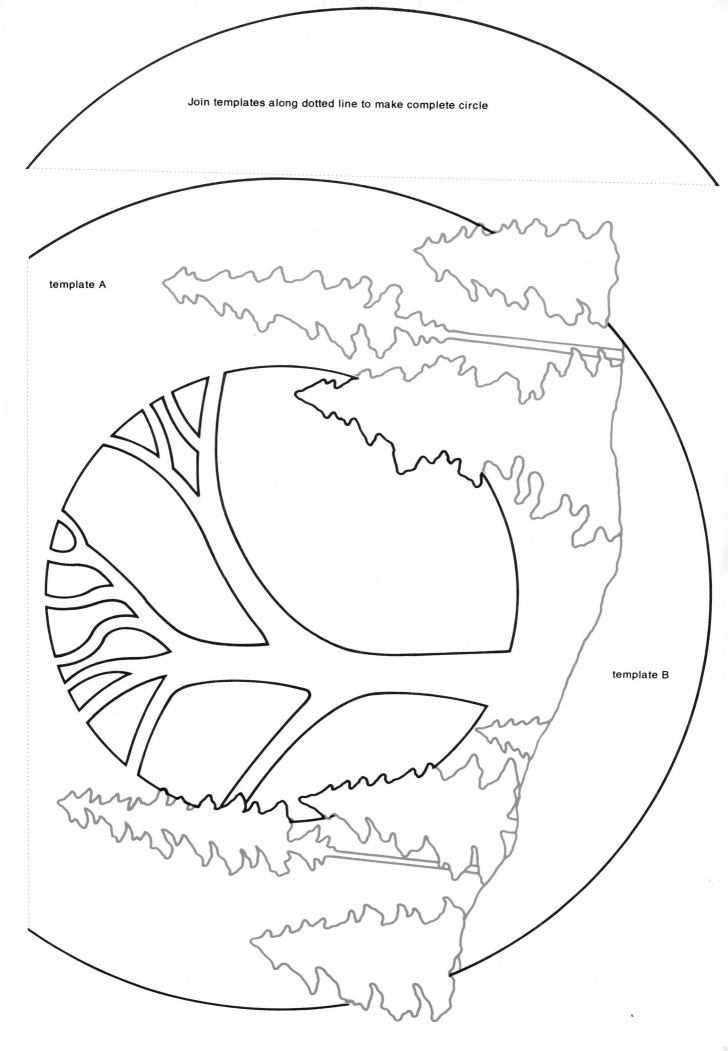

Join templates along dotted line to make complete circle

template A

template B

PLAQUE

Scribe the picture onto the plaque, but keep the scribing to a minimum, only outline the bridge and houses and roughly mark on the position for each tree.

When painting on sugarpaste, keep the brush fairly dry as too much water will melt the sugar. Before adding colour, make a paper circle the same size as the moon on the drawing and place in position on the plaque. Use a large brush first of all to apply the yellow colour to the sky. Deepen the tone slightly for the bridge and apply a fairly strong, warm yellow for the lighted window. Warmth can be added to the yellow by mixing with a little orange colouring.

When the yellow colouring has dried, apply the lilac-blue tones. Starting again with the pale areas, paint in the snow foreground and roofs and gradually deepen the tone for all the shadow work. Draw in the trees with a very fine brush. Lastly, when the branches are dry, dust the outer area of the trees with a lilac-grey dusting powder.

Remove the paper circle from the plaque. The moon should shine out as a dazzling disc of white.

Lastly, attach the collar to the top of the cake with royal icing and apply the run-out snow border. Dust the cake with lilac and warm yellow dusting colours, using the photograph as a guide, to give depth to the finished cake. Lastly attach the trees to the base border.

template C

snow border

base border

62

INGREDIENTS

20cm (8in) round fruit cake
boiled, sieved apricot jam (jelly)
900g (2lb) marzipan
1.8kg (4lb) sugarpaste
cornflour (cornstarch)
non-toxic silver colouring
grape, claret, blue, green, yellow and skintone
*   paste colours*

EQUIPMENT

30 × 35cm (12 × 14in) oval cake board
pastry brush
crimper No2
scalpel
tracing paper
paintbrushes Nos 000, 1, 2
large rolling pin
small rolling pin

CRIMPING

This is an easy technique which beginners can soon master and one which produces a professional finish to the cake. Crimping is also a great way to disguise poor surfaces such as of cracks, accidental indentations and air bubbles. It is important to practice on a spare piece of sugarpaste to discover how many different effects and designs can be achieved by using the combination of various crimping and indenting tools.

To ensure that the crimpers do not spring open when in use, which could tear the paste, twist an elastic band around the head of the tool. Dip the head into cornflour (cornstarch) to prevent the crimper from sticking to the paste. Insert the crimper into the paste and pinch together. Release slowly and withdraw the crimper. The paste can be easily torn or pulled away from the surface of the cake if this process is rushed.

Crimping is mostly done on a freshly covered cake so that the surface is still soft and malleable. However, with this particular cake, it has been covered with white sugarpaste and allowed to skin. Bands of coloured sugarpaste have then been applied on top of the white sugarpaste. The edges of these bands have then been decorated by the use of a scalpel and the base of a piping tube which would have marked the surface of the cake were this not already dry and firm.

PREPARING THE CAKE

Carve away the top edge of the cake to create a rounded, domed shape, keeping it as rounded and smooth as possible. Model an extended point at the base of the bauble using marzipan taking care to keep the join smooth. Cover the entire cake with marzipan. The modelled base of the bauble and the rounded area of the cake should now appear as one shape. Cover the resulting cake with white sugarpaste and allow the surface to harden.

Colour 225g (8oz) sugarpaste to a deep pink using claret paste colouring. Colour a further 225g (8oz) of paste lilac using grape colouring. Measure across the cake using a piece of string. Draw a band as long as the measurement taken and 3cm (1½in) wide, curving the top and bottom edges of the band so that when it is applied to the bauble it will create a three-dimensional effect. Using the grape-coloured sugarpaste, roll out a strip of paste and cut out the curved band using your template. Using the diagram provided as a guide, place the band on the bauble in the appropriate place. Smooth and trim away any excess at the cake edge. Use a No2 crimping tool to crimp near the top and bottom edge. Using a scalpel, cut away the excess paste near the crimped edge to give a smooth scalloped look.

Roll out the pink-coloured sugarpaste. Make a pattern and cut out a 3cm (1½in) strip as for the previous band and again, using the diagram as a guide, place in an appropriate position on the cake. Crimp the scalloped pattern and trim as before. For the bottom edge, use the base of a piping tube to create the scalloped edging.

Between these two bands, apply the two angels in the stages and colours as shown. Measure the centre point between the two angels and apply a cut-out star in white modelling paste. Continue to add the grape and pink bands using the pattern as a guide.

Cover the cake board with sugarpaste coloured a bluish green. This is more easily achieved by rolling out a strip of sugarpaste, cut one edge straight and gently roll up. Place the joining edge at the bottom of the bauble where the area between the edge of the bauble and the edge of the board is quite narrow. Carefully unroll the strip butting the straight cut edge to the side of the cake. Where the two joining edges meet, smooth gently with the hand to eradicate the joining line. Trim away the excess paste at the edge of

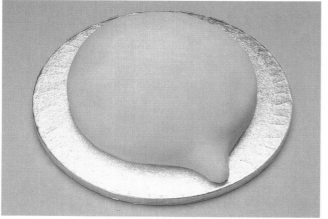

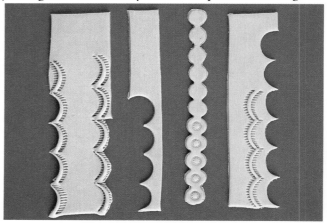

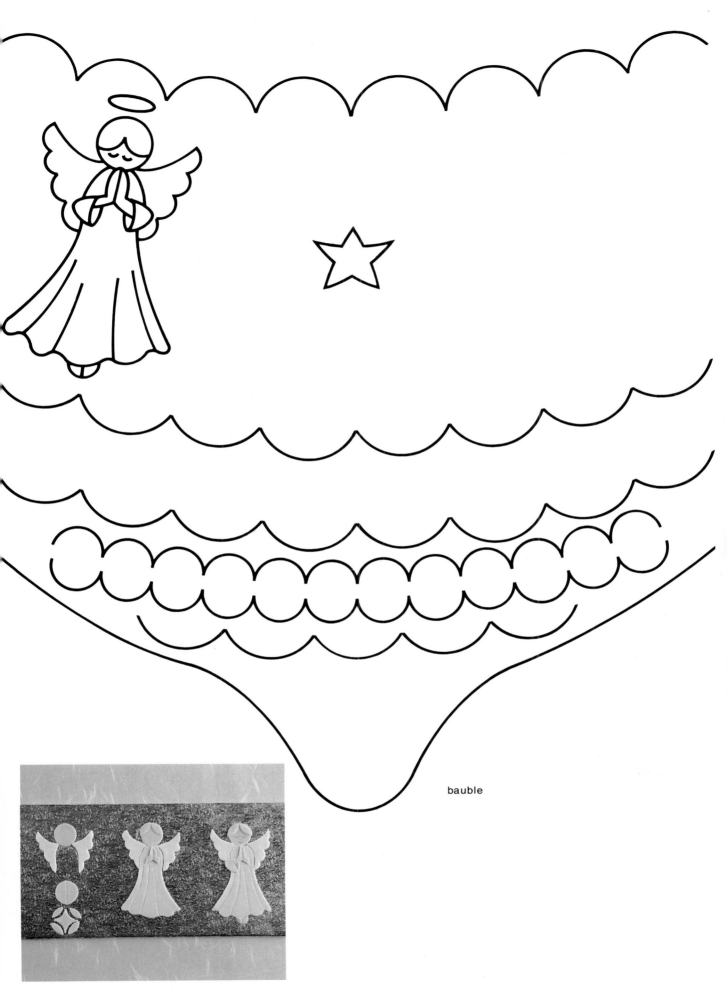

bauble

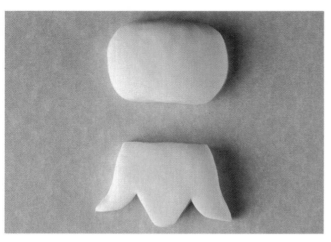

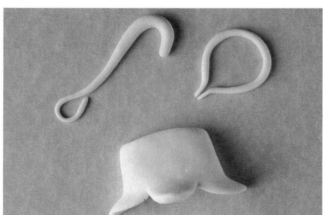

the board. When the paste is dry, paint small silver stars onto the base with a fine brush.

BAUBLE TOP

Mould a 75g (3oz) piece of white sugarpaste into a rectangular shape. Round off the corners and, using the template provided, cut out the shape of the top. Round off the cut edges with the fingers smoothing the ends of the points so that they curve upwards until they fit snugly onto the curved shape of the bauble. Make a hole at the top edge fairly near the board so that the ring will fit inside.

RING AND HOOK

Roll a piece of modelling paste into a thin rope and form into a circular shape as shown. Leave to dry, then place into the hole at the top of the bauble and secure with royal icing.

For the hook, make an elongated rope which gradually tapers at one end. Place the tapered end through the attached ring and close to form another ring. Curve the thicker end into a hook shape and support with foam until dry.

When dry, paint the top, ring and hook with non-toxic silver paint.

Add the finishing touches to the angels with a fine brush and add the nose, lips and eyes. Darken the inside of the sleeve with a darker shade of grape. Darken the wings near the body. Paint the stars between the angels with the silver paint.

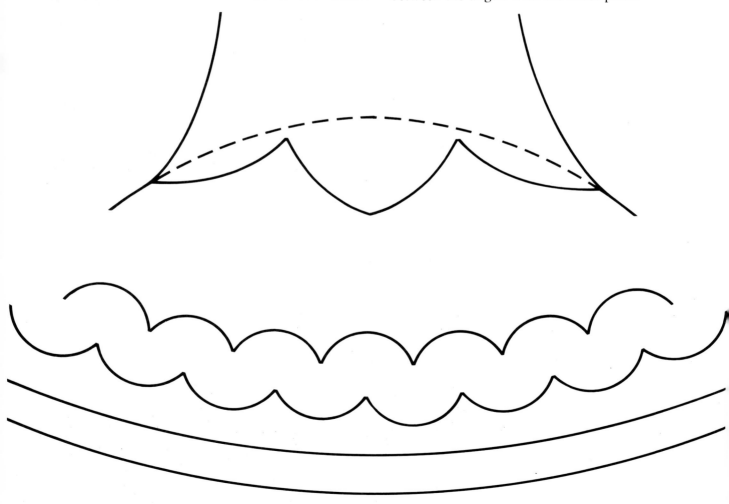

INGREDIENTS
12.5 × 17.5cm (5 × 7in) rectangular fruit cake
boiled, sieved apricot jam (jelly)
675g (1½lb) marzipan
675g (1½lb) sugarpaste
550g (1¼lb) modelling paste
assorted paste and dusting colours
gum arabic glue/glaze
egg white
small quantity royal icing
cornflour (cornstarch)

DECORATIONS
small offcuts thin red ribbon
1 metre (1 yard) red ribbon

EQUIPMENT
21 × 26cm (8½ × 10½in) cake board
pastry brush
large and small rolling pin
scalpel
modelling tools
paper tissue
firm, thin card
scriber
florist's wire
paintbrushes Nos 0000, 0, 1, 2
glue brush
clay gun
vegetable parchment piping bag
clean dishcloth

Cover the cake with marzipan and sugarpaste in the usual way. Make a pillow by moulding a 75g (3oz) piece of sugarpaste into a smooth rectangular shape rounded at the edges and corners. Gently pull out each of the four corners with the fingers to give it a pillow-like appearance. Make indentations with a large ball tool for the child's teddy and doll's head. Place at one end of the cake. Make sure that the pillow does not overhang the cake at all because at a later stage the bed head will be placed against the side of the cake.

CHILD'S HEAD
For the child's head, roll a small ball of paste into a small plum shape. Slice away the back half of the head. Smooth the cut edges and round with the fingers. Form the features by indenting the eye socket with a ball tool. Remember to exaggerate these indentations as modelling paste is later applied. Pull out a small piece of paste on the side edge to form a small nose. Place the head into the largest indentation on the pillow.

THE BODY
To get the proportions of the child's body correct, bear in mind that for a child the body should be between four and five times as big as the head. Make the torso and legs as shown. Exaggerate the form so that the contours of the shoulder, waist and hip are extreme. When the blanket is placed over the figure these contours will be less obvious. Make a crude arm shape and attach to the shoulder.

BLANKET
Use a large tissue to measure the size of the blanket. Drape the tissue over the figure of the child and bed and trim it to the correct size. Round off the bottom two corners so that the paste will fall neatly to the board edge. Remove the tissue and use it to make a template from the card. Roll out 650g (1½lb) sugarpaste to 5mm (⅛in) thickness, cut around the card and smooth the cut edges.

Drape the paste over the sleeping figure and the bed. Arrange the folds at the two bottom corners so that they fall neatly. Smooth the blanket over the sleeping form so that the shape of the body becomes more obvious. Leave to dry. When dry, use a scriber to mark the squares of the patchwork onto the blanket. Paint on the patterns using a fine brush. Make sure each background colour is dry before adding any surface pattern such as stripes, spots or flowers. Keep the brush as dry as possible as too much wetness will cause the sugar to melt. Avoid overbrushing when colouring the background square colours as this could cause streaking.

FACE, DOLL AND TEDDY
Apply the face using skin-coloured modelling paste and the template. The technique used is the same as for the bas relief angel on page 33.

Colour 25g (1oz) of paste with a pale chestnut

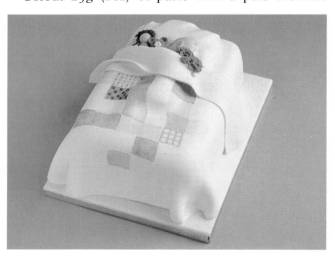

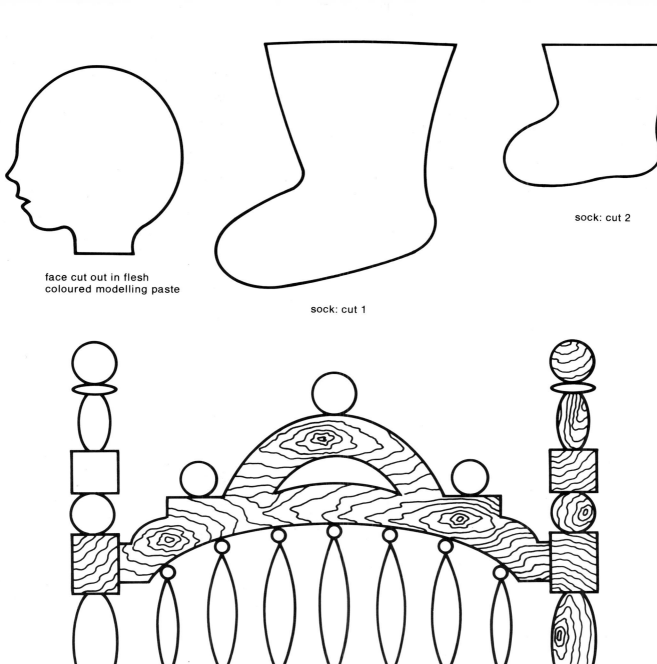

face cut out in flesh
coloured modelling paste

sock: cut 2

sock: cut 1

colour for the teddy bear. Only his head and one paw will be visible so attention to detail is unnecessary.

For the head, make a small ball, indent two small holes with a ball tool for the eyes. Roll two small balls of paste and insert into the sockets. Make a small pea-sized shape for the muzzle in white paste. Attach with glue and indent a hole for the nose. Place a small ball of black paste into the indentation. For the ears, make two pea-sized balls of paste and flatten between the fingers. Place on a piece of foam and indent with a ball tool to cup. Place onto the head with gum arabic glue. Roll a small sausage shape for the arm. Flatten the end slightly for the paw and curve the arm. Make a rough oval shape for the body. Place the head and body onto the pillow and bed and glue the arm in position.

For the doll, roll a small ball of flesh-coloured paste for the head, make this roughly the size of a small grape. Make an oval shape for the body in blue paste. Place in position on the bed. Make a small sausage for the arm. Wrap a small piece of blue paste around the upper arm. Attach the arm to the body.

SHEET TOP
Use the upper part of the blanket template and cut out a strip of modelling paste the width of the bed by 7.5cm (3in). Thin the cut edges that will be visible with a large ball tool. Apply the glue to the long edge that has not been thinned. Lay the strip near to the neck of the child and across the bed, glued side down

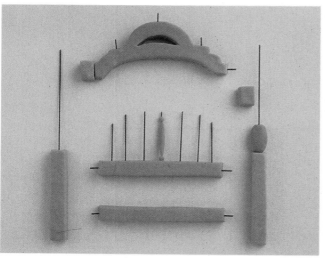

and fold the strip back onto itself to form the roll. Drape the paste over the sleeping figure. Slightly twist the ends of the strip that are near the board to give a natural appearance.

HAIR AND FEATURES
Soften some modelling paste with egg white and force through a clay gun. Starting with the curls at the bottom end of the hair, gradually work up the child's head and finally around her face. Drape the hair over the pillow and over the sheet. Make hair for the doll and apply in the same way. For the teddy's fur, pipe royal icing, coloured to match the teddy's body, over the face and shoulders of the bear and, with a stiff brush, texture the surface.

Paint in the features on the doll, emphasize the sleeping eyes by painting a line underneath the small balls of paste on both the teddy's and the girl's eyes. Paint in the eye lashes. Paint small circles for the doll's cheeks in pink and a tiny rosebud mouth. Dust the child's cheeks lightly with a touch of peach or skintone dusting powder. Paint in some stitching on the part of the doll's dress that is visible.

BED HEAD
Colour about 450g (1lb) modelling paste a light chestnut colour. Roll the paste out to about 6mm ($\frac{1}{4}$in) and cut out two pieces of paste to represent the wood running across the base of the bed and the two upright pieces that will form the legs. Push some firm florist's wire through these pieces. To assemble, use modelling paste mixed with a little gum arabic to form a soft, sticky paste.

Start to assemble the bed by joining the one upright strut with the two horizontal struts. Use the template as a guide, and cut out the squares and form the large and small balls. Thread onto the wire in the order shown. When the large ornate upper section has been completed, the second upright strut is then attached. Complete the top part of the bed, again using the diagram as a guide.

Once the bed is dry, using a fine brush, paint on the wood grain pattern in a deeper chestnut colour. When completed, glaze the bed head using gum arabic glaze. When dry, attach to the top side of the bed.

For the final finishing touches, cut out the socks from red paste using the template provided. Dust the cut shapes lightly with cornflour (cornstarch) and press into a clean dishcloth. The weave on the cloth will give the socks a knitted look. Apply a little gum arabic to the inner edge of the sock and roll back the edge. This will produce a rounded, three-dimensional look. Attach to the end of the bed. Repeat for the smaller socks.

Make a small Christmas decoration to hang on the bed head by rolling a small ball of white paste and inserting holly, Christmas roses and red ribbon loops into the ball. Place a small red bow at teddy's neck. Attach a red ribbon around the board edge.

Note: As wire has been used in this cake, a warning must always be given to the recipient so that the items can be removed from the cake before eating.

INGREDIENTS

20cm/8in oval fruit cake
boiled, sieved apricot jam (jelly)
900g (2lb) marzipan
900g (2lb) sugarpaste
50g (2oz) modelling paste
deep cream, brown, grape, claret, yellow, green,
*   red, orange and black paste colours*
brown dusting powder
small quantity royal icing
gum arabic

DECORATIONS

6 holly leaves and berries (see page 10)
1 metre (1 yard) thin red ribbon
1 metre (1 yard) thin orange ribbon

EQUIPMENT

30cm (12in) oval cake board
pastry brush
large rolling pin
small rolling pin
scalpel
vegetable parchment piping bags
piping tube No1
glue brush
paintbrushes Nos 0, 1
modelling tools
palette knife
tracing paper
thin firm card

Cover the cake in the usual manner, first with marzipan and then with sugarpaste coloured to a deep shade of cream with paste colour; leave to dry.

Cut out two sections for the window using the template provided. Cut out the frame in paste coloured to a pale, brown, stone colour and the glass from white paste. Use the base of a piping tube to cut out the circular shape at the top of the window frame.

When dry, colour the glass by painting with pale grape claret, warm yellow and green paste colours. Paint irregular shapes over the glass blending each colour into the next so that there are no definite lines dividing each coloured section. Use a new, finely pointed food colour brush to apply the black lines.

Position the window on the cake and attach with royal icing. Apply the window frame on top of the coloured glass and again attach with royal icing.

Cut out bricks in the same coloured paste as the window frame and attach around the window.

Colour a grape-sized piece of paste brown for the branch. Roll out into a long rope and lay on top of the template bending and pinching into shape. Cut to size and attach to the cake with gum arabic glue.

ROBINS

The robins are applied to the cake in the order marked on the template. Trace the shape of the first robin then mould a piece of white modelling paste until it fills the drawn outline. If the paste stands too high off the paper, remove and with a sharp knife, cut a slice from the underneath then re-apply to the tracing paper. Shape the bird using a modelling tool as shown.

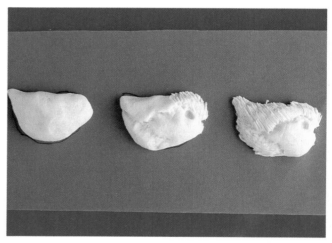

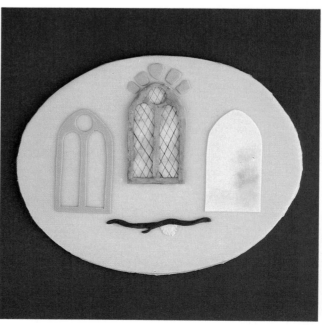

Depress the paste underneath the wings and brown part of the cap.

Indent the eye sockets and mouth with a small ball tool. Depress the paste under the breast until it is quite thin where it will touch the branch. While the paste is still soft and pliable, mark the texture with a sharp scalpel. Start at the head and work gradually over the back, wing and tail, then proceed under the eye sockets, down over the breast to the underside of the bird. When the texturing has been completed, slide a palette knife under the bird and transfer to the cake surface. Before adding the other two birds, make the tail for the second bird and the wing for the third; position on the cake and attach with gum arabic.

When the birds are dry, paint in the cap, wings and back with brown paste colour taking care to work the colour into the textured surface so that no white paste shows through. Apply red colour around the eyes and on the upper breast area. Gradually work orange into the red so that there is no definite line between the two colours. Tone the colour down to a lighter shade of orange at the lower breast area. Leave the underside of the bird white.

Roll some small balls of black paste for the eyes and shape a small piece of brown paste, (leftover from the branch) into a flattened triangular shape. Place in the mouth for the upper beak, repeat for the lower beak. Paint the inside of the mouth with a darker brown paste colour. Make six feet from small rolled strands of brown paste and attach with gum arabic.

Dust the bricks around the window with a slightly darker brown tone near the window edge.

Mix the royal icing to a soft consistency and apply to represent snow on the upper edge of the bricks, window ledge, window panes and on the heads of the birds. Make small dots of royal icing over the surface of the cake for the snowflakes.

Make the holly and berries as described on page 10 and attach to the cake. Paint on the musical notes using a fine paintbrush and black paste colour.

Finish the cake by attaching two bands of thin ribbon at the base of the cake in orange and red to blend with the colours on the cake. Apply a small bow to each band as shown.

FATHER CHRISTMAS IN A SLEIGH

INGREDIENTS

20cm (8in) round fruit cake
boiled, sieved apricot jam (jelly)
900g (2lb) marzipan
900g (2lb) sugarpaste
100g (4oz) modelling paste
blueberry and assorted paste colours
opaque white colour
gum arabic

DECORATIONS

1 metre (1 yard) thin red ribbon
1 metre (1 yard) thicker red ribbon to go around board

EQUIPMENT

30cm (12in) round cake board
pastry brush
large rolling pin
small rolling pin
scalpel
glue brush
paintbrushes Nos 0000, 0, 1
cranked palette knife
tracing paper
thin, firm card for templates

This is a time consuming cake to make, but not a difficult one.

Cover the cake in the usual manner with marzipan followed by the sugarpaste coloured to a deep blue with blueberry blue paste colour. Leave to dry and

form a reasonably firm skin.

Using the template provided, make two complete tracings of the design, one to use as a pattern guide to cut out the paste shapes and the second to act as an accurate guide when placing the cut shapes in position. For example, when the two lead reindeer are cut out, the tracing, minus the reindeers, can be placed on the cake. The cut out paste reindeer are then simply applied to the cake surface through the cut out area.

Roll the modelling paste fairly thinly, but not too thin – it should still have some body to it. Place the traced pattern shape on top of the rolled out paste and, using a sharp scalpel, cut around the card cleanly. Apply each shape carefully to the top of the cake with gum arabic glue using the second template as a guide. Cut and apply all the required shapes in this manner.

When cutting out the two lead reindeers, cut out as one shape and separate the two forms by indenting the outline between them.

When all the basic shapes of the design have been applied, add the colour. Prevent the colours running by allowing one colour to dry before painting in an adjacent shape. Begin by painting the reindeers light brown using paste colours. Where the fur is white, leave the paste unpainted. Add the subtle shadows and tones by carefully blending brown dusting colour onto the painted area. Make sure that all the excess powder has been knocked off the brush before applying to the cake so that it does not adhere to other parts of the cake surface. Continue painting until all the necessary cut out pieces have been coloured.

Add the finishing touches on the reindeers. The red harnesses and reins should be made using thin strips of paste. Cut out the two flat runners using the templates provided and attach to the cake. For the scroll work, roll a very fine piece of paste with the fingers until it resembles a fine piece of twine. Using the template as a guide, place the rolled paste on top of the drawn scroll work and flatten with the fingers. Remove the flattened shape very carefully with a palette knife. Glue and attach between the runner and the edge of the sleigh. Complete all the scroll work in this way. Add the darker red border to the sleigh and add the holly wreath. Paint the holly and berries onto the dry wreath. Paint on the features of Father Christmas.

Using opaque paint and a fine brush, paint tiny stars all over the deep blue background colour. When dry, paint the white stars a bright yellow. Apply depth to the cloud shapes by using a blue dusting colour in a swirled pattern.

Apply a thin, red ribbon band at the base of the cake taking care to pick out the same red as used on the cake surface. Add a wider red ribbon in the same shade to the edge of the cake board.

Join templates along dotted line to
make complete circle

INGREDIENTS

20cm (8in) round fruit cake
boiled, sieved apricot jam (jelly)
900g (2lb) marzipan
900g (2lb) sugarpaste
175g (6oz) modelling paste
assorted paste colours
skintone and red and dusting colours
small quantity of royal icing
gum arabic

DECORATIONS

holly leaves (see page 10)
1 metre (1 yard) thin red ribbon
1 metre (1 yard) thicker red ribbon to go around
  board

EQUIPMENT

30cm (12in) cake board
pastry brush
large rolling pin
small rolling pin
scalpel
vegetable parchment piping bags
tracing paper
No 2 piping tube
glue brush
paintbrushes Nos 000, 0, 1
modelling tools
thin, firm card for templates
small pieces of foam

Cover the cake with marzipan and sugarpaste in the usual way. Colour some modelling paste to a deep green colour. Make a rough tracing of the basic shape of the wreath. Cut out a card pattern and place on the rolled out paste. Cut out using a sharp scalpel, place in position on top of the cake and glue into a place using gum arabic glue.

FATHER CHRISTMAS

Colour some modelling paste deep red and roll out to about 3mm (⅛in) thick. Using the template as a guide, place the pattern on the red paste and cut out the main body shape of Father Christmas. Roughly indent a shape where the arm is to be placed, this allows the arm to fit naturally into the body.

Using sugarpaste, create a flattened ball shape on top of the traced pattern of the head of Father Christmas using the outline of the head as a guide. Trim off any excess paste to give some shape to the flattened ball. Remove the finished shape from the tracing paper and transfer it to the cake surface. Colour a small pea-sized ball of modelling paste to a skintone colour. Roll out and apply to the face area. Smooth the paste with the fingers, making sure that the skintone paste completely covers the sugarpaste on the side edge where it meets the cake surface. Indent the eyes and nose with a ball tool. Roll two small balls of white paste for the eyes and one larger ball in skintone for the nose, glue in place.

For the hat, roll a piece of red paste about the size of a grape first into a ball and then into a cone. Flatten

and place onto the sugarpaste head. Add some creases with a modelling tool to create a natural look.

To make the arm, roll a thick sausage shape in red modelling paste. Bend it in half and flatten the back so that it will fit neatly into the indented shape. Using a modelling tool, open up the cuff area just enough to place the hand inside. Make the hand from a ball of red paste. Flatten the ball into a spade shape, curve the hand slightly at the point where it has been flattened. Roll the opposite edge so that it will fit inside the cuff. Glue into position.

Pipe fur around the cuff and hat using royal icing and texture by stippling the surface with a small, stiff brush. Paint on the eyes. Dust the cheeks with a deeper skintone colour and dust the nose to create a reddish hue.

Push some white modelling paste through a clay gun for the beard. Add a small moustache and the eyebrows. Indent a small shape under the moustache for the mouth. When the paste is dry, paint or dust this area in a skintone colour for the mouth. Colour a small pea-sized piece of paste black. Roll out into a thin strip and attach to his waist for the belt.

REINDEER

To make antlers, roll out a thin sausage shape in white modelling paste. Snip into the sausage using a scalpel or a fine pair of scissors. Push the cut shape away from the sausage and rotate it between the fingers. Make a further cut and rotate in the same way, as shown. Place the roll onto a tracing of the antlers and bend the paste into shape using the template as a guide. Cut off any excess paste and leave to dry. Make a further fifteen antlers in this way.

For the head, use white paste to roll a large pea-sized ball of paste, flatten. Form a point at one end for the nose and place on the template as a guide for shape and size. Indent two holes for the eyes. Then, make two holes in the top of the head into which the now dried antlers can be positioned and glued in place. Roll out a small piece of white paste for the ears and cut out using the pattern provided. Indent and flatten the lower part of the ear as shown. Glue and attach to

the underside of the head. Repeat for the other ear.

When dry, paint the face and lower ear light brown. In a darker shade of brown, paint the top of the head and the upper ear. Dust the antlers a light brown colour. Make two small balls in black paste for the eyes and place into the eye sockets. Glaze with gum arabic when dry. Paint in a small teardrop shape for the nose.

Make eight reindeers in total and attach to the cake surface either side of the Father Christmas using the template as a positioning guide.

PARCELS

Make some squares, rectangles and rolled shapes. Cut off the back, lower, underside corner at an angle so that when the parcels are placed on the cake surface they will tilt slightly forwards, creating a feeling of perspective. Paint a pattern on each parcel using paste colours and a fine brush. Cut out very thin strips of paste and place around the parcels. Add small bows to finish. Attach the parcels to the garland using a little royal icing.

BOW

Colour some modelling paste a deep red. Using the pattern provided, cut out the shape marked A and attach to the garland as shown. Cut out the two ribbon ends and soften all cut edges with a ball tool to give some shape to the two ties. Place in position. Cut one bow shape, again, soften the cut edges. Roll the shape in half to form a loop and glue in place. Support the loop with a small piece of foam until the paste is dry. Repeat for the opposite loop. For the knot, mould a ball of red paste, flatten the underside and add a few creases and folds with a modelling tool. Place in the centre of the two loops.

Make the holly leaves as shown on page 10. Attach around parcels, reindeer and Father Christmas with royal icing. Using a No2 piping tube, pipe red berries onto the holly.

Attach a thin ribbon around the base of the cake in the same shade as the paste bow. Attach the thicker ribbon to the edge of the cake board.

bow

A